Grade Five

Music Theory

4th Imprint

(ABRSM 2020-present Syllabus)

GRADE FIVE MUSIC THEORY COURSE AND EXERCISES

By Victoria Williams

www.mymusictheory.com

Copyright © 2020 Victoria Williams

All rights reserved.

4th Imprint

ISBN-13: 978-1530154685

ISBN-10: 1530154685

INTRODUCTION

This book was written for students who are preparing to take the ABRSM Grade Five Music Theory exam. Parents of younger students will also find it helpful, as well as busy music teachers who are trying to fit a lot of music theory teaching into a very short time during instrumental lessons.

This updated edition has been revised to reflect minor changes to the ABRSM syllabus which were effected in 2018 and 2020.

Each topic is broken down into digestible steps, and for best results the lessons should be followed in the order they are presented, as the acquired knowledge is cumulative.

After each topic, you will find a page or so of practice exercises, to help you consolidate what you have learned. Answers are provided on the page following the exercises.

At the end of the book there is a practice test which is in a similar style to the actual exam papers.

I also highly recommend purchasing ABRSM past papers before sitting an actual exam. These can be obtained from shop.abrsm.org, Amazon or your local sheet music reseller.

You are welcome to photocopy the pages of this book for your own use, or to use with your pupils if you are a music teacher.

ABOUT THE AUTHOR

Victoria Williams graduated with a BA Hons degree in Music from the University of Leeds, UK, in 1995, where she specialised in notation and musicology. She also holds the LmusTCL and AmusTCL Diplomas in Music Theory from Trinity College London.

You can connect with Victoria Williams in the following ways:

www.mymusictheory.com

info@mymusictheory.com

www.facebook.com/mymusictheory

www.twitter.com/mymusictheory

https://www.youtube.com/user/musictheoryexpert

CONTENTS

Introduction 5
1. Notation 7
2. Foreign Terms 19
3. Time Signatures 30
4. Clefs 51
5. Key Signatures 58
6. Scales 64
7. Intervals 83
8. Transposing 93
9. Chords 102
10. Progressions and Cadences 112
11. Instruments 123
Grade 5 Music Theory Practice Test 129
Appendix – SATB & Composition 138

1. NOTATION

WHAT IS NOTATION?

Notation is the system of symbols we use in order to write down music so that other people can play it.

Notation is made up of the stave, notes, rests, bar lines, markings for tempo, dynamics and phrasing, clefs, indications of key and time, ornaments and other indications which can be for specific instruments, like how to use a bow, pedal or mute.

For your grade 5 theory exam, you'll need to understand all of the common notation symbols. You should also learn how to **handwrite** music in a clear and readable way, as it is very useful in real life!

You probably already know most of the common symbols, as you'll have come across them in the music you've been playing or singing up to now. This lesson is a collection of all the symbols you need to know- try testing yourself to make sure there aren't any gaps in your knowledge before you take your exam!

Some items need more detailed study, and there are complete lessons available on them later in the book. You'll find foreign language terms in the next lesson.

Tip! When handwriting music, always use a pencil. Choose one which is dark and easy to rub out, and make sure it is sharpened!

NOTE VALUES

Each different shape of note has a name and a value. The notes have different names in the UK/Australia compared to those in use in the USA. The ABRSM exam papers will use both versions, as will this book. You can choose to use whichever set of names you prefer.

Below you'll find the main note values in order, with their names, starting with the longest note value.

Each note is worth **half** the value of the note before it in the list. So, a crotchet (quarter note) is worth 2 quavers (eighth notes), and a minim (half note) is worth 4 quavers (eighth notes) and so on.

When counting out notes, we normally assign the value of "one" to a crotchet (quarter note). The numbers below the stave show the relative values of each note.

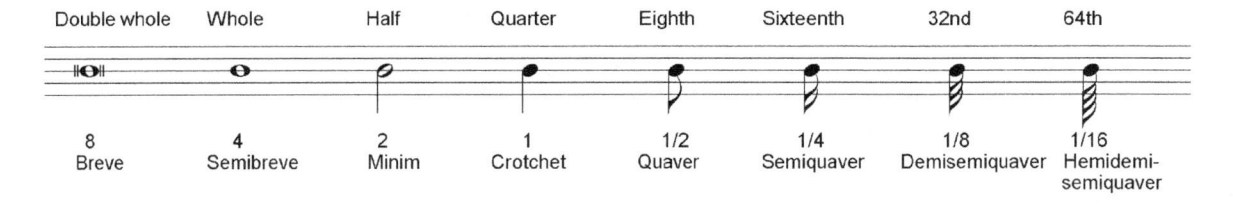

Double whole	Whole	Half	Quarter	Eighth	Sixteenth	32nd	64th
8	4	2	1	1/2	1/4	1/8	1/16
Breve	Semibreve	Minim	Crotchet	Quaver	Semiquaver	Demisemiquaver	Hemidemi-semiquaver

Dotted Notes and Pauses

Notes can have one or two dots placed after them. A dot increases the value of the note by 50%, or in other words the value is the "note plus **half** of the note". So, a dotted crotchet (dotted quarter note) is equal to 1.5 counts, and a dotted minim (dotted half note) the same as 3 counts.

A second dot increases the value of the note by 75%, or "the note plus **half** of the note, plus **quarter** of the note". So, a double dotted crotchet (double dotted quarter note) is worth 1.75 counts. A double dotted minim (double dotted half note) is worth 3.5 counts.

Notes can be tied together, with a curved line. The values of tied notes should be added together and played without a break. Only notes of exactly the same pitch can be tied together. Ties are often seen across bar lines.

Any note value can be increased by a short but indefinite amount of time with the use of the **pause** (also called "fermata") symbol:

The pause is usually placed above the stave, but is also sometimes seen below it, in which case, it is drawn the other way up:

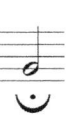

For Grade 5 Theory, you need to know all the names, and the values each note represents. You'll need to be able to calculate the values of several different notes added together.

Rests

Rests work just like notes in notation, except of course you don't have to play anything when there is a rest! Here are the rests, in the same order as the notes were written above.

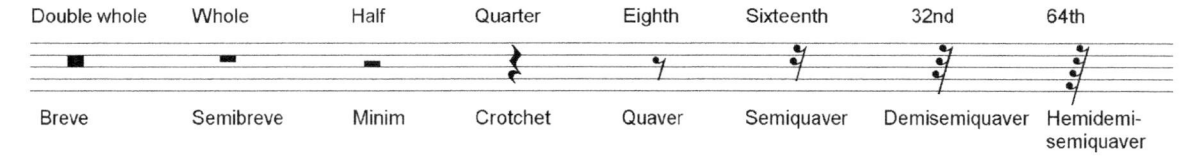

Double whole	Whole	Half	Quarter	Eighth	Sixteenth	32nd	64th
Breve	Semibreve	Minim	Crotchet	Quaver	Semiquaver	Demisemiquaver	Hemidemi-semiquaver

Rests can be dotted in exactly the same way as notes can, but dotted rests are normally only found in compound time signatures (i.e. those with 6, 9 or 12 as the top number – more on this later!)

If you can't remember whether the minim (half) rests hang off or sit on the line, try to remember it this way: "4 is higher than 2"- so a 4-beat rest is higher up the stave than a 2-beat rest. Semibreve (whole) rests hang off the second line from the top, while minim (half) rests sit on the middle line. All other rests should be placed more or less centrally on the stave, (except where you have multiple parts on one stave - see Lesson 9.)

The semibreve (whole) rest can be used to show a **complete bar** of rest in any time signature (except 4/2 which needs 2 of them). The whole bar rest is placed in the middle of a bar.

Bar lines and Navigating through a Piece of Music

Bar lines help you when you're reading music because they break the music up into small chunks which take up the same length of time

Bar lines are also used to divide longer music up into sections, and to show you which bars to repeat, if any. (The USA word for "bar" is "measure").

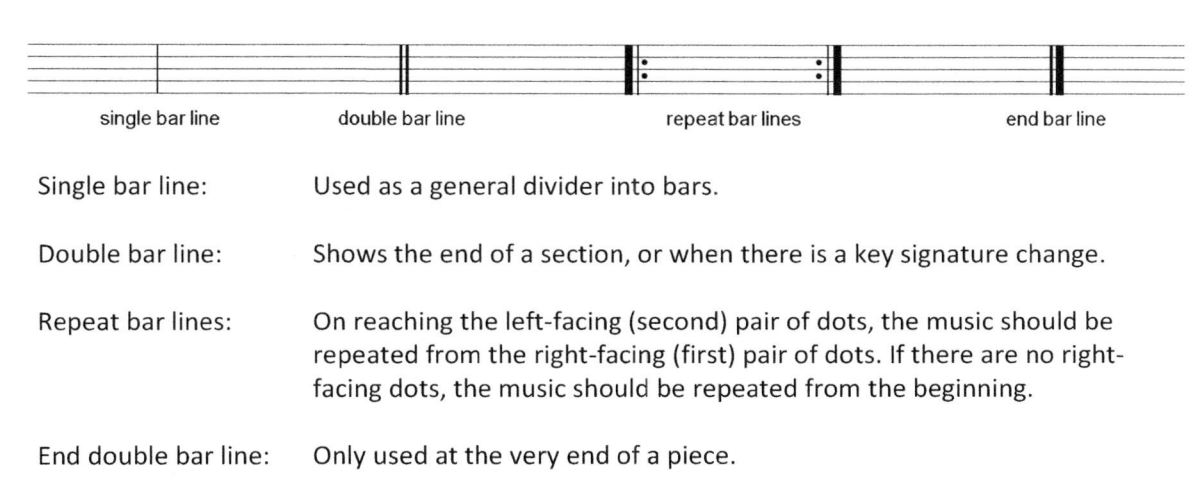

| single bar line | double bar line | repeat bar lines | end bar line |

Single bar line: Used as a general divider into bars.

Double bar line: Shows the end of a section, or when there is a key signature change.

Repeat bar lines: On reaching the left-facing (second) pair of dots, the music should be repeated from the right-facing (first) pair of dots. If there are no right-facing dots, the music should be repeated from the beginning.

End double bar line: Only used at the very end of a piece.

Other symbols are used to help you navigate your way through the score. You need to know that "Da" and "Dal" mean from (the), and "Al" means to (the).

D. C.   D.C. stands for Da Capo, which means "from the head"; or in other words, go back to the beginning.

D. S.   D.S. stands for Dal Segno (pronounced SEN-yo), which means "from the sign"; or go back to the sign.

𝄋   Sign (segno). This is the "sign" referred to by D.S.

al Coda   Play until you see the Coda sign.

𝄌   Coda sign. Jump from here to the Coda (at the end of the piece), which will also be marked with this sign.

al Fine   Play until the end.

The symbols above are used together to create precise instructions. You might see "Dal segno al fine" (go back to the sign and then play till the end), or "Da capo al coda" (go back to the beginning, play until you see the coda sign, then jump to the coda at the end of the piece).

You can see that using the Italian abbreviations is much shorter than the English!

Clefs

You need to know about the **treble**, **bass**, **alto** and **tenor** clefs for Grade 5 Theory. The clefs are covered in detail in Lesson 4.

Key Signatures and Time Signatures

Key and time signatures are a big deal, and there's quite a lot to learn about them. You can find a whole lesson on key signatures in Lesson 5, and on time signatures in Lesson 3.

Ornaments

Ornaments are special symbols written into music to make it sound more decorated. They occur mostly in music from the Baroque, Classical and Romantic eras. Ornaments are always written above the stave. Here's a summary, with a notated example of how each one is played. You'll need to recognise both the symbol, and the written-out form (but you won't be asked to write them out).

Trill (rapid movement between the note itself and the note above)

Appoggiatura (a-po-ja-TU-ra) – (takes about half of the time of the note itself)

Upper mordent (the note itself and the note above)

Lower mordent (the note itself and the note below)

Acciaccatura (a-cha-ka-TU-ra) (a "grace note" – squeezed in before the note itself)

Turn (or "upper turn" the note above, the note itself, the note below)

Tempo

The tempo (or speed) of a piece of music is shown at the beginning of the piece, and changes might occur during the piece. Tempo can be indicated with **words** (see Lesson 2 – Foreign Terms for the grade 5 terms), or **symbols**. Using symbols, tempo is indicated with a note value and the metronome marking it requires, for example like this:

♩ = 60

A metronome marking of 60 means 60 clicks per minute (or one every second).

Dynamics

Dynamics (or volume) can be indicated either in **words** (see Lesson 2 – Foreign Terms for all the terms you need to know for grade five), with **abbreviations** of those words, or with **symbols**.

Immediate changes in dynamics are usually indicated with abbreviations:

pp	Pianissimo	Very quietly
p	Piano	Quietly
mp	Mezzo piano	Moderately quiet
mf	Mezzo forte	Moderately loud
f	Forte	Loud
ff	Fortissimo	Very loud

In addition, you might see *sf* or *sfz* which stand for "sforzando" and means play one note very loudly, and *fp* which means play loudly, but then immediately make the note quiet.

Gradual changes in dynamics are often shown with hairpins like this:

Crescendo: gradually get louder

<

Decrescendo: gradually get quieter

>

Hairpins are more precise than words because they can show more exactly where the change in dynamic starts and finishes.

Phrasing and Articulation

Music for all instruments can be phrased. Phrase marks are curved lines which group together notes which belong in one phrase, like this:

Individual notes can be played in a huge number of ways, and so there are several "articulation" indications to show what you need to do. Some articulation indications only apply to certain instruments, while others are pretty much universal.

Here are the main articulation markings:

staccato   staccatissimo   tenuto   accent   marcato

Staccato: Detached (distinctly separated from the next note), and short.

Staccatissimo: Extremely detached and short.

Tenuto: Hold the note for its full length.

Accent: Attack the note with extra force.

Marcato: Accent the note.

When a note has no specific articulation marking on it at all, its articulation depends on the instrument. If there are no markings for a wind or brass instrument it means the note should be "tongued", and for a string player it means "bowed".

Pedals, Bows and Mutes.

Many instruments employ extra bits and pieces to further the range of sounds they can produce. Pianos have got either 2 or 3 pedals, brass and string instruments can use mutes, and most string instruments can be played with either a bow or the fingers.

Pedal Marks

All pianos have a left and a right pedal.

On a grand piano, the left pedal reduces the volume by causing only one string to be hit instead of the normal three, and is called "una corda", meaning "one string" (think of "one cord").

On an upright piano the mechanics are a little different, but the overall effect is similar. This pedal is often referred to as the "soft pedal".

The right pedal is called the "damper" or "sustain" pedal, and causes the strings to continue vibrating after the keys have been released. (Some people call this the "loud" pedal, but that's not the right name for it!)

Grand pianos have a third pedal, called the "sostenuto" pedal (don't confuse this with "sustain" pedal!) This enables the player to let the sound continue on some notes, but for other notes to be unaffected.

There is no standard way to mark pedal indications for the piano, but here are some accepted methods, all of which are written below the grand staff:

𝓟𝑒𝑑.	Press the damper (right) pedal.
✻	Release the damper pedal.
Una corda (u.c.)	Press the una corda (left) pedal.
Tre corde (t.c.)	Release the una corda pedal (literally, this means "three strings").

How to Write Neat Music

Writing good, clear notation is really important. Although you won't need to write music by hand in the online theory exam, it's still a really good skill to learn.

Follow these guidelines to help you write beautiful manuscript:

- All notes have a head, most have a stem, and some have a tail.
- Breves and semibreves (double whole and whole notes) only have a head.
- Minims and crotchets (half and quarter notes) have a head and a stem.
- Quavers (eighth notes) and all smaller notes have a head, a stem and a tail.
- Note heads are not perfectly round they are oval.
- Make the stems of your notes the same length. As a rough guide, a note written in the bottom space should have a stem which reaches up to the top line:
- Notes on ledger lines should have stems which reach to the middle line of the stave.
- Crotchets and minims (half and quarter notes) written below the middle line should have stems up, written above the middle line should have stems down. If they are written on the middle line itself, they should follow the stem direction of the notes next to them.
- Tails on quavers (eighth notes) and smaller notes are on the right side of the stem.
- Sharps, flats and naturals (accidentals) are always written immediately to the left of the note they affect. Accidentals need only be written once within a single bar.
- Use a ruler to draw stems and beam lines neatly.
- Leave a slight space after the bar line before placing your first note. Don't put a bar line on the left edge of a single stave.
- Left edge lines are only used when two or more staves are bound together, for example in piano music.
- Space out your notes relatively to one another. Give a minim (half note) more space than crotchet (quarter note), and so on.
- Spacing is good. The minim (half note) has about twice as much space as the crotchet (quarter note):

- Spacing is wrong. The minims and crotchets (half and quarter notes) have been given the same amount of space and the quavers (eighth notes) have more space than the longer notes. The minims (half notes) should have a big space after them, the crotchets (quarter notes) should have a medium space, and the quavers (eighth notes) should have the smallest space after each one.

NOTATION EXERCISES
Name or explain the following symbols.

NOTATION TEST 1

1. [short trill/mordent above quarter note]
2. *Ped.*
3. *t.c.*
4. [grace note before half note]
5. [crescendo hairpin]
6. [fermata over three notes]
7. [coda sign]
8. [staccato eighth rest/notes]
9. [note below staff]
10. ♩ = 60
11. [trill/mordent above note]
12. [final barline]
13. 𝄋 (segno)
14. ❋ (pedal release)
15. [repeat sign]
16. ♪
17. **ff**
18. [note with marcato below]
19. ∧ [marcato above note]
20. [two notes]

Notation Test 2

Draw/write each of the following indications, using the appropriate words or symbols.

1.	Staccato		11.	Breve (double whole) rest	
2.	Trill		12.	Release the damper (right) pedal	
3.	Minim (half) rest		13.	Pause	
4.	Demisemiquaver (32nd) note		14.	Double bar (end of section)	
5.	Go back to the start		15.	Very quietly	
6.	Gradually getting softer		16.	One note suddenly loud	
7.	Press the damper (right) pedal		17.	Moderately loud	
8.	Staccatissimo		18.	Coda sign	
9.	Crotchet (quarter) rest		19.	Semibreve (whole) rest	
10.	Accent		20.	Breve (double whole) note	

NOTATION ANSWERS
Notation Test 1 Answers

1.		Lower mordent	11.		Upper mordent
2.	Ped.	Right (sustaining) pedal	12.		End of piece
3.	*t.c.*	Release the left (soft) pedal	13.	𝄋	Sign
4.		Acciaccatura	14.	✻	Release the right (sustaining) pedal
5.		Gradually getting louder	15.		Repeat section
6.		Turn	16.	♪	Quaver (8th note)
7.		Coda	17.	*ff*	Very loud
8.		Hemidemisemiquaver (64th) rest	18.		Staccatissimo – very short and detached
9.		Tenuto (hold for full length)	19.		Marcato – accented
10.	♩=60	Metronome marking	20.		Appoggiatura

Notation Test 2 Answers

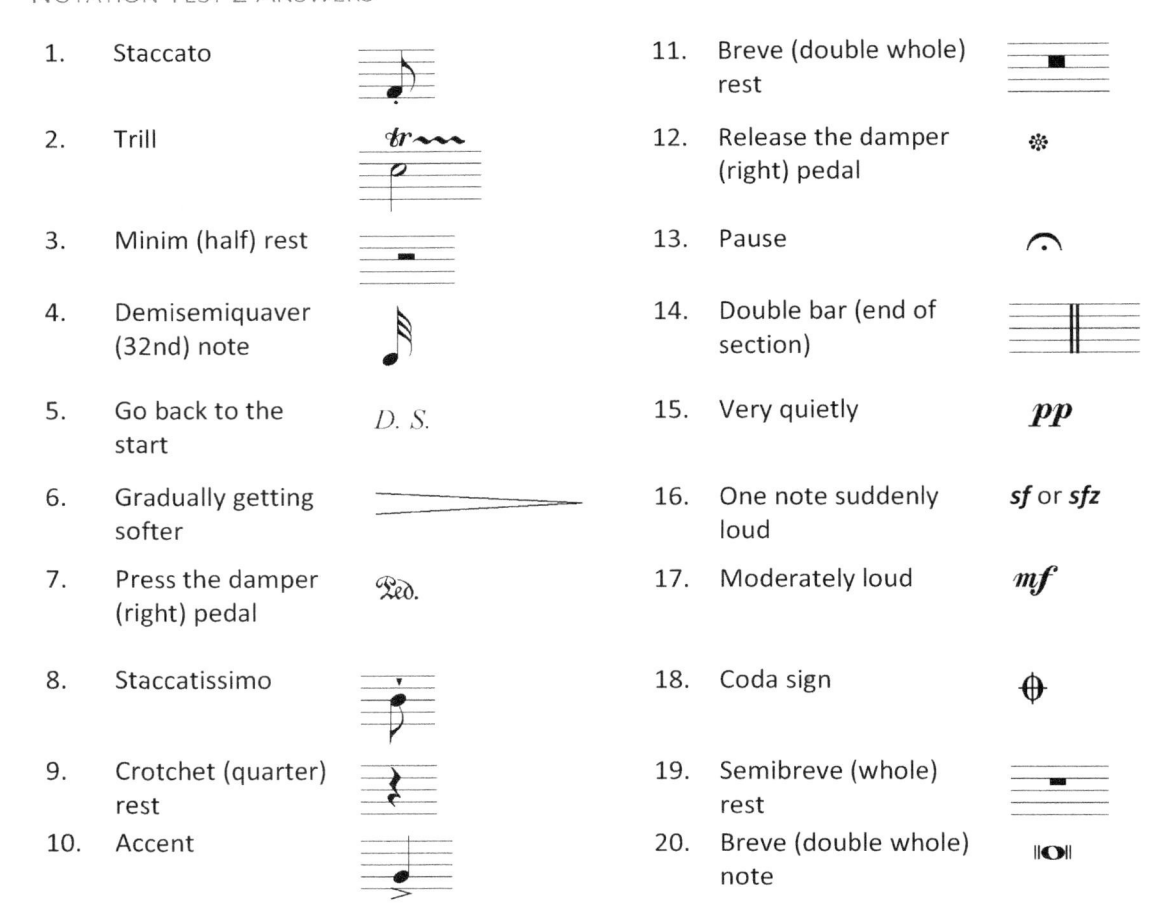

1.	Staccato		11.	Breve (double whole) rest		
2.	Trill		12.	Release the damper (right) pedal		
3.	Minim (half) rest		13.	Pause		
4.	Demisemiquaver (32nd) note		14.	Double bar (end of section)		
5.	Go back to the start	*D. S.*	15.	Very quietly	***pp***	
6.	Gradually getting softer		16.	One note suddenly loud	***sf*** or ***sfz***	
7.	Press the damper (right) pedal		17.	Moderately loud	***mf***	
8.	Staccatissimo		18.	Coda sign		
9.	Crotchet (quarter) rest		19.	Semibreve (whole) rest		
10.	Accent		20.	Breve (double whole) note		

2. FOREIGN TERMS

For Grade 5 Theory, you need to try to learn all the foreign terms listed below. (This list includes all the terms from grades 1-4, which you will also need to know!)

In this lesson you will find the Grade 5 music theory terms grouped together. They are grouped by type and by language.

The groups are dynamics, tempo, articulation (attack), expression and "other". The words in the "other" group are mostly grammatical words, like "not", "very", "less" and so on. Grammatical words are usually used with words from the other groups; in a direction like "allegro assai", "allegro" means fast, so it's in the "tempo" group, but "assai" means very, so it is in the "other" group.

Most foreign musical terms are Italian, but there are also some French and German terms too.

Try learning one group at a time. (There are too many words to try to memorize them all in one go!)

It is worth knowing that the endings of Italian words often hold a clue to their meaning. Words ending in "–ando" or "-endo" usually translate to "-ing" in English, and so refer to a gradual change. The ending "-issimo" intensifies the meaning of a word, like the word "very". Words ending in "-ino" or "-etto" add the meaning of "a little bit".

Dynamics (All dynamic terms are Italian)

Fortepiano – loud then immediately soft

Morendo – dying away

Niente – nothing (=silence)

Perdendosi - dying away

Smorzando – dying away in tone and speed

Crescendo (cresc.) – gradually getting louder

Decrescendo (decresc.) – gradually getting softer

Diminuendo (dim.) – gradually getting softer

Forte (f) – loud

Mezzo forte (mf) – moderately loud

Fortissimo (ff) – very loud

Piano (p) – soft

Mezzo piano (mp) – moderately soft

Pianissimo (pp) – very soft

Tempo (Italian)

General Tempo Words

Tempo – time

A tempo – in time

Rubato – with freedom of time

Slow Tempo Words

Adagio – slowly

Largo – Slow and stately

Larghetto – Rather slow

Lento – Slow

Grave – Very slow and solemn

Allargando – Broadening

Rallentando (rall.) – gradually getting slower

Ritardando (rit.) – gradually getting slower

Ritenuto (rit.) – gradually getting slower

Smorzando – dying away in tone and speed

Moderate Tempo Words

Andante – at a walking pace

Andantino – slightly faster than andante

Comodo – comfortably

Moderato – at a moderate speed

Quick Tempo Words

Allegro – fast

Allegro assai – very fast

Allegro moderato – moderately fast

Allegretto – Fairly quick

Presto – Very fast

Vivace – Lively and quick

Vivo – Lively and quick

Agitato – agitated

Stringendo – gradually getting faster

Accelerando – getting faster

Tempo (French)

Lent – slow

Retenu – held back

Modéré – moderate speed

Vite – quick

Tempo (German)

Langsam – slow

Mässig – at a moderate speed

Lebhaft – lively

Schnell - fast

Articulation (all terms are Italian)

Sforzando – forced, accented

Sforzato – forced, accented

Tenuto – held for the full value

Marcato – emphatic, accented

Sotto voce – in an undertone

Staccato – short and detached

Staccatissimo – very short and detached

Expression (Italian)

Happy words

Dolce – sweetly

Semplice - simply

Amabile – pleasant

Grazioso – graceful

Tranquillo – calm

Giocoso – playful

Scherzando – playfully, joking

Romantic words

Affettuoso – tenderly, affectionately

Appassionato – passionately

Spirited Words

Animato – animated, lively

Energico - energetically

Deciso – with determination

Maestoso – majestically

Risoluto – bold, strong

Lyrical Words

Cantabile – in a singing style

Cantando – singing

Sonoro – resonant, with a rich tone

Sad Words

Dolore – grief

Doloroso – sorrowful

Mesto – sad

Tristamente – sadly

Triste – sad

Non-emotional Words

Espressivo - expressive

Largamente – broadly

Sostenuto – sustained

Legato - smoothly

Leggiero – lightly, nimbly

Pesante – heavy

Rinforzando – reinforcing

Ritmico – rhythmically

Expression (French and German)

Animé (Fr.) – animated

Douce (Fr.) – sweetly

Ruhig (Ger.) – peaceful

Traurig (Ger.) – sad

OTHER (ITALIAN)

Al, alla – in the style of

Assai – very

Ben – well

Come – as, similar to

Con, col – with

E, ed – and

Ma – but

Meno – less

Mezzo – half/moderately

Molto – extremely

Mosso – movement

Non – not

Più – more

Poco – a little

Primo, prima – first

Quasi – as if, resembling

Sempre – always

Senza – without

Simile (sim.) – in the same way

Subito – suddenly

Troppo – too much

FOREIGN TERMS EXERCISES
Foreign Terms Test 1

Give the English meaning of the following foreign musical terms.

1. A tempo
2. Accelerando (accel)
3. Ad libitum (ad lib.)
4. Adagio
5. Affettuoso
6. Agitato
7. Al, alla
8. Alla breve
9. Allargando
10. Allegretto
11. Allegro
12. Allegro assai
13. Allegro moderato
14. Amabile
15. Andante
16. Andantino
17. Animato
18. Animé
19. Appassionato
20. Assai
21. Attacca
22. Ben
23. Brio
24. Cantabile
25. Cantando
26. Come
27. Comodo
28. Con, col
29. Crescendo (cresc.)
30. Da capo (d.c.)
31. Dal segno (d.s.)
32. Deciso
33. Decrescendo (decresc.)

Foreign Terms Test 2

Give the English meaning of the following foreign musical terms.

1. Diminuendo (dim.)
2. Dolce
3. Doloroso
4. Douce
5. E, ed
6. Energico
7. Espressivo
8. Fine
9. Forte (f)
10. Fortepiano (fp)
11. Fortissimo (ff)
12. Forza
13. Giocoso
14. Grave
15. Grazioso
16. Langsam
17. Largamente
18. Larghetto
19. Largo
20. Lebhaft
21. Legato
22. Leggiero
23. Lent
24. Lento
25. Ma
26. Maestoso

Foreign Terms Test 3

Give the English meaning of the following foreign musical terms.

1. Marcato
2. Marziale
3. Mässig
4. Meno
5. Mesto
6. Mezzo
7. Mezzo forte (mf)
8. Mezzo piano (mp)
9. Moderato
10. Modéré
11. Molto
12. Morendo
13. Mosso
14. Niente
15. Non
16. Perdendosi
17. Pesante
18. Pianissimo (pp)
19. Piano (p)
20. Più
21. Poco
22. Presto
23. Prima, primo
24. Quasi
25. Rallentando (rall.)
26. Retenu
27. Rinforzando (rf, rfz)
28. Risoluto
29. Ritardando (rit.)
30. Ritenuto (rit.)
31. Ritmico

Foreign Terms Test 4

Give the English meaning of the following foreign musical terms.

1. Rubato
2. Ruhig
3. Scherzando
4. Schnell
5. Semplice
6. Sempre
7. Senza
8. Sforzando (sf)
9. Sforzato (sfz)
10. Simile (sim.)
11. Smorzando
12. Sonoro
13. Sostenuto
14. Staccato (stacc.)
15. Stringendo
16. Subito
17. Tempo
18. Tenuto
19. Tranquillo
20. Traurig
21. Tristamente, Triste
22. Troppo
23. Vite
24. Vivace, vivo

FOREIGN TERMS ANSWERS

Foreign Terms Test 1 Answers

1. In time
2. Gradually getting faster
3. At choice
4. Slow
5. Tenderly
6. Agitated
7. In the style of ...
8. With a minim (half note) beat
9. Broadening
10. Fairly quick
11. Fast
12. Very fast
13. Moderately fast
14. Amiable, pleasant
15. At a walking pace
16. Slightly faster than andante
17. Animated, lively
18. Animated, lively
19. With passion
20. Very
21. Go immediately to next section
22. Well
23. Vigour
24. In a singing style
25. Singing
26. As, similar to
27. At a comfortable speed
28. With
29. Gradually getting louder
30. Repeat from beginning
31. Repeat from "S" sign
32. With determination
33. Gradually getting quieter

Foreign Terms Test 2 Answers

1. Gradually getting quieter
2. Sweet, soft
3. Sorrowful
4. Sweet
5. And
6. Energetic
7. Expressive
8. The end
9. Loud
10. Loud, then immediately soft
11. Very loud
12. Force
13. Playful, merry
14. Very slow, solemn
15. Graceful
16. Slow
17. Broadly
18. Rather slow
19. Slow and stately
20. Lively
21. Light
22. Light, nimble
23. Slow
24. Slow
25. But
26. Majestic

Foreign Terms Test 3 Answers

1. Emphatic, accented
2. In a military style
3. At a moderate speed
4. Less
5. Sad
6. Half/moderately
7. Moderately loud
8. Moderately quiet
9. Moderate speed
10. Moderate speed
11. Very much
12. Dying away
13. Movement
14. Nothing (silence)
15. Not
16. Dying away
17. Heavy
18. Very quiet
19. Quiet
20. More
21. A little
22. Fast (faster than allegro)
23. First
24. As if, resembling, like
25. Gradually getting slower
26. Held back
27. Reinforcing
28. Bold, strong
29. Gradually getting slower
30. Held back
31. Rhythmically

Foreign Terms Test 4 Answers

1. With some freedom of time
2. Peaceful
3. Playfully, joking
4. Fast
5. Simple, plain
6. Always
7. Without
8. Forced, accented
9. Forced, accented
10. In the same way
11. Dying away in tone and speed
12. Resonant, with a rich tone
13. Sustained
14. Short and detached
15. Gradually getting faster
16. Suddenly
17. Speed, time
18. Held
19. Calm
20. Sad
21. Sorrowful
22. Too much
23. Quick
24. Lively, quick

3. TIME SIGNATURES

You might also like our series of video tutorials on time signatures and related exam questions:

https://www.youtube.com/playlist?list=PLyZpSAfmPoZET8BagwvG6xA1qb1eQhuzN

A time signature is a symbol that has two numbers, one on top of the other.

The time signature is written at the beginning of a piece of music. Often, a piece of music will stay in the same time signature all the way through, but some music also contains changes of time signature. The time signature is always written after the key signature (or clef, is there is no key signature).

BEATS AND DOWN BEATS

The time signature is there to tell you **how to count the beats** in the music. The beat, or "pulse" is the steady unit of time which you can clap along to, tap your foot to, or march with. Most of the time the beat does not get faster or slower, but sometimes it can speed up or slow down for a special effect. A metronome is a tool which can be used to hear a steady beat while you play music. Orchestras and bands usually employ a conductor, so that all the players can keep to the same beat.

Conductors, (and some metronomes) also indicate the **down beat**. The down beat is the first beat in each bar. The down beat is played with a little accent, or extra weight, compared to the other beats in the bar. Because it stands out a little bit, we are able to understand how many beats there are in a bar when we listen to music. If none of the beats in the bar was accented, we would not be able to tell the difference between the various time signatures.

Compare these two tunes. They both have the same notes and rhythms in them, but they are in different time signatures. The time signature affects the way the music sounds, because we hear a different accented note in each bar in 3/4 compared to 4/4. The down beats are shown by the accented notes (this is just to help you see them).

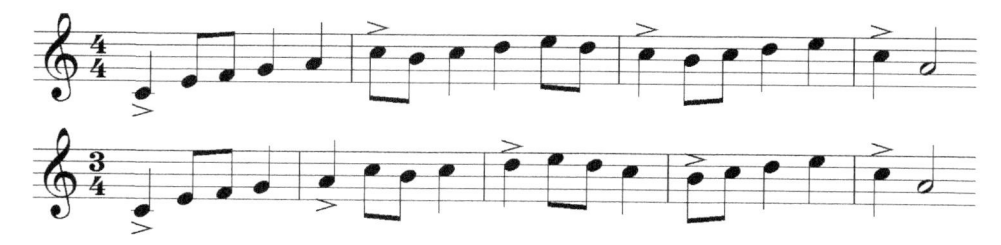

When words are sung to music, we usually sing accented syllables with the strong beats in the bar, and unaccented syllables with the weak beats. Try saying these words out loud, and notice how the strong syllable in each word lines up with the first beat in each bar. In a word, it is not always the first syllable which is accented.

el - e - phant   ti - ger   rhi - no - cer - us   gi - raffe

Duple, Triple and Quadruple, Regular and Irregular

If there are two beats per bar, we call this **duple time**. Three beats per bar is **triple time** and four beats per is called **quadruple time**.

The vast majority of music (both classical and popular) falls into one of these three types. We call these **regular** time signatures.

A small number of other pieces of music have different patterns, for example 5, 7, 10 or 11 beats per bar. These are called **irregular** time signatures.

We do not normally think of music as having 6, 8, 9 or 12 beats per bar (even though you might see these numbers in time signatures). This is because these numbers can be halved or divided into three, to make *regular* time signatures.

- 6 = duple time (6÷3=2)
- 8 = quadruple time (8÷2=4)
- 9 = triple time (9÷3=3)
- 12 = quadruple time (12÷3=4)

The irregular time signatures cannot be divided by 2 or 3 to arrive at a duple, triple or quadruple time signature (10÷2=5, for example).

Rhythm and Beat

The beat is a steady, unchanging pulse, like the ticking of a clock.

Rhythm is a changeable element of music – it can be quick or slow.

Here is an exercise you can try, to help understand the difference.

Start tapping your foot at a steady, medium pace – about once per second. Now clap your hands at the same time. When you are ready, double the speed of your claps: clap twice as fast as you are tapping your foot – two claps for each foot tap. Your foot is still tapping the **beat**, but your hands are now clapping a **rhythm**.

Now trying clapping four times with each foot tap. Try varying your claps to one per beat, two per beat, and four per beat.

Now try to clap three times per foot tap. You might find this a little bit trickier than the first exercise at first, but with a little practice it should become easier.

In music, rhythm is created by using notes of different lengths. Sometimes the notes might be the same length as the beat of the music. At other times they might be faster, or slower.

Dividing the Beat

In the previous exercise we tried to clap twice for each foot tap. This is dividing the beat into **2**. We also tried to clap three times per foot tap. This is dividing the beat into **3**.

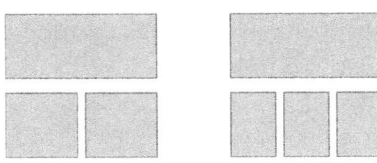

Time signatures that normally divide the beat into two are called **simple** time signatures. Those that divide the beat into 3 are called **compound** time signatures.

We also tried to clap 4 times per foot tap – this is the same as dividing by 2, then dividing by 2 again, so it is also a **simple** time signature.

Time Signatures

We have learned that most music is **duple**, **triple** or **quadruple** (2, 3 or 4 beats per bar). We have also learned that time signatures can be **simple** or **compound**. This gives us six basic patterns for time signatures. We can have 2, 3 or 4 beats per bar, and those beats can divide into either 2, or 3:

Pattern	Beats	Time Signatures	Name
	2 beats, divided into 2	2/4 and 2/2	Simple duple
	3 beats, divided into 2	3/8, 3/4 and 3/2	Simple triple
	4 beats, divided into 2	4/8, 4/4 and 4/2	Simple quadruple
	2 beats, divided into 3	6/8 and 6/4	Compound duple
	3 beats, divided into 3	9/8 and 9/4	Compound triple
	4 beats, divided into 3	12/8 and 12/4	Compound quadruple

Length of the Beat

For each pattern, there is more than one possible time signature. For example, in simple duple time, we find the time signatures 2/4 and 2/2.

The difference between these time signatures is only in the length of note used for the beat. There is no real difference in the way 2/4 and 2/2 sound – the difference is only in the way they are written.

Very generally, slow moving music is more likely to use a longer note value for the beat, and faster music is more likely to use a faster note value for the beat. There are plenty of exceptions however.

The **lower** number in the time signature tells you what type of note to count as the beat.

Lower number	Simple time signatures beat =	Compound time signatures beat =
2	Minim (half note)	-
4	Crotchet (quarter note)	Dotted minim (dotted half note)
8	Quaver (8th note)	Dotted crotchet (dotted quarter note)
16	Semiquaver (16th note)	Dotted quaver (dotted 8th note)

Here are some examples.

Time signature	Type	Beat	Example
4/4	Simple Quadruple	Crotchet (Quarter note)	
4/2	Simple Quadruple	Minim (Half note)	
3/8	Simple Triple	Quaver (8th note)	
3/2	Simple Triple	Minim (Half note)	
6/8	Compound Duple	Dotted crotchet (Dotted quarter note)	
6/4	Compound Duple	Dotted minim (Dotted half note)	

BEAMING

Notice that quick notes (quavers/8th notes and faster) are grouped together with a beam. Each group will add up to one whole beat, or multiples of whole beats. This helps you see where the beats in the bar are. For example, in 4/4 time, we have two grouped quavers (8ths):

and four grouped semiquavers (16ths)

Each group adds up to one crotchet (quarter note) beat.

In 6/8, the beat is a dotted crotchet (dotted quarter note), so we see three grouped quavers (8th notes):

Sometimes a rest might be part of a group which makes up a whole beat:

In simple time signatures, you should beam together notes which add up to multiple beats, but only if they are all the **same type** of note, and that note is worth **half a beat**.

If the notes are worth **less than half** of a beat, they should be grouped in single beats (otherwise they become difficult to read).

If the notes are of different values, they should be grouped in single beats too.

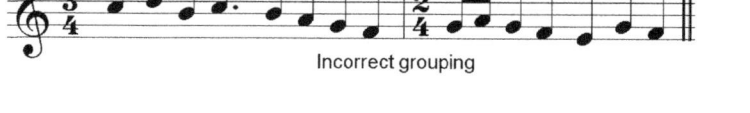

In 4/4 time, you should group quavers (8th notes) into two whole beats, but only across beats 1-2 and beats 3-4. You may not group them across beats 2-3. This is because beat 3 is the second strongest beat in the bar in 4/4 time, and it should be easy to see where in the bar it lies. 2/2 works in the same way.

The stems of beamed notes normally should all point in the same direction. The correct direction is that which is right for the note in the group which is **furthest away from the middle line.**

Sometimes either direction will work. In this example, C and A are the same distance from the middle line:

In irregular time signatures there is no standard way to group the notes. The grouping will depend on which notes in the bar the composer wants to be accented. In the example below, the first bar emphasises beats 1 and 4, whereas in the second bar the emphasis is on beats 1 and 5. We can describe the grouping as "3, 4" followed by "4,3".

Triplets and Duplets

Although the beat in simple time signature normally divides into two, we can also make it divide into three. Similarly, in a compound time signature it is possible to divide the beat into two.

When the beat is divided into three instead of two, we use a **triplet.** A triplet is shown by a "3" symbol. It means "play three notes in the time of two". Triplet quavers (8th notes) are slightly faster than normal quavers.

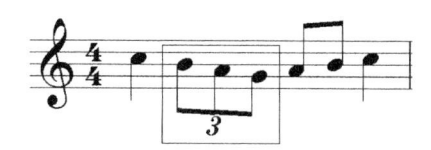

If the beat is a minim (half note), we can use three crotchets (quarter notes) to make a triplet, which is equal to one beat. (When triplets are made with notes that cannot be beamed, use a bracket to show which notes belong to the triplet.)

If the beat is a quaver (8th note), we can use three semiquavers (16th notes) to make a triplet.

Triplets can also be made using a combination of note values. This triplet uses a crotchet (quarter note) and quaver (8th note). Compare this bar to the previous 4/4 bar.

Rests can be included within triplets.

In compound time when the beat is divided into two instead of three, we use a **duplet.** A duplet is shown by a "2" symbol. It means "play two notes in the time of three". The duplet quavers (8th notes) in these examples would be played slightly slower than the normal quavers.

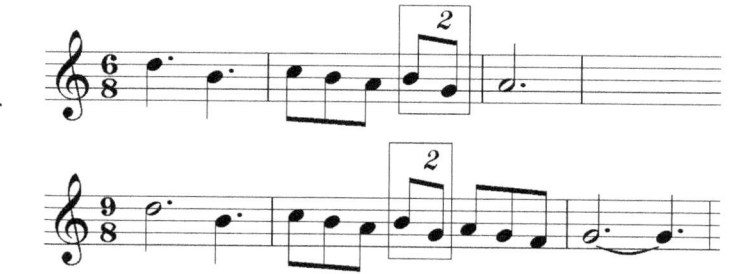

Ties

Ties are used to join beats together. They make it easier to see where the beats in the bar fall, compared to using notes which hide the beats. In 4/4 time for example, it is important to be able to see where the third beat of the bar is, because it is an emphasised beat. The **second** of the tied notes shows where a new beat starts.

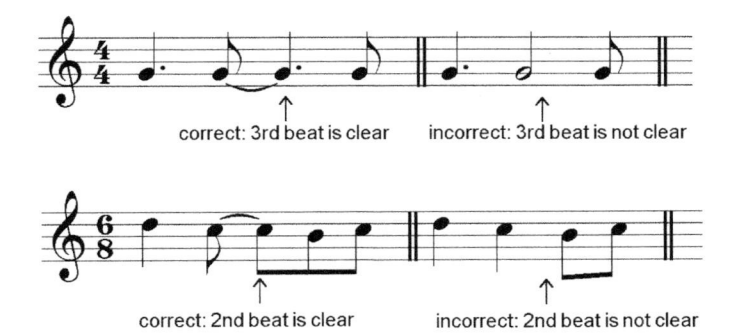

correct: 3rd beat is clear   incorrect: 3rd beat is not clear

correct: 2nd beat is clear   incorrect: 2nd beat is not clear

Summary of Time Signatures

Simple Time

- Top number is 2 (duple), 3 (triple) or 4 (quadruple)
- Main beat is split into 2
- Notes are grouped in 2s or 4s
- Main beat is not a dotted note
- Triplets might be used

Compound Time

- Top number is 6 (duple), 9 (triple) or 12 (quadruple)
- Main beat is split into 3
- Notes are grouped in 3s
- Main beat is a dotted note
- Duplets might be used

ADDING BAR LINES TO A MELODY

In this type of question, you are given a short melody with the time signature. You need to work out where the bar lines should go. You will normally be told whether the melody starts on the first beat of the bar.

To solve this type of question, you just need to **add up the note values** then put in bar lines to make complete bars. (The last bar might not be a complete bar – if it is **not** complete, don't add a bar line at the end).

Here's a typical question (which starts on the first beat of the bar):

Look at the **lower** number in the time signature. This tells you the kind of note to count up:

= count minims (half notes)

= count crotchets (quarter notes)

= count quavers (eighth notes)

Next look at the upper number. This tells you **how many** of those notes are needed in each bar.

Count out the required number of notes, then draw a bar line. Repeat, until you get to the end. Double check the length of the final bar, and a final bar line only if it is complete.

In the above melody, the time signature is 6/8. This means each bar needs to have the equivalent of six quavers (8th notes). Pay attention to the way the notes are beamed - you will **never** draw a bar line through a beamed group. Tied notes are often (but not always) either side of a bar line.

Have a go at putting the bar lines in place in the above melody, then compare your answer below.

Working Out the Time Signature

In an exam question asking you to find the correct time signature, it is not enough to simply count up the notes and rests in the bar.

You will need to work out whether the time signature should be **duple, triple or quadruple**, and also whether it is **simple or compound**, to get the right answer.

Compare these three melodies. They all contain the same total number of notes/rests (the equivalent of 6 crotchets (quarter notes).

What are their time signatures?

Melody a is in 3/2 time. Although the first bar could be divided into either two or three beats, the second bar makes it clear that there are three beats. It is triple time, so it is 3/2.

Melody b is in 6/4 time. The second bar is arranged differently now: there are clearly two equal halves, so this is duple time.

Melody c is in 12/8 time. The choice of note values in bar 1 shows that one beat equals a dotted crotchet (dotted quarter note). In particular, the ties show us where beats 2 and 4 begin. In bar 2, we can see four beats quite easily.

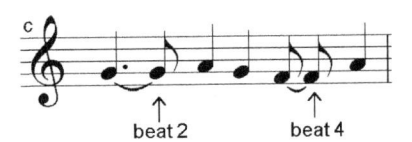

Here is an example question.

The following melody requires a different time signature in each bar. Add the correct time signatures.

Follow the steps below.

1. Try to divide the bar up into **2 or 3** equal beats.
   - If you find you cannot, because there are e.g. 5 or 7 beats in the bar, then simply count those beats and write in the time signature e.g. 5/4 for "5 crotchets" (quarter notes).

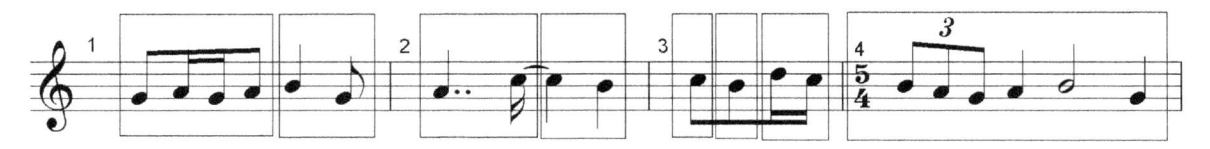

   - Bar 1 = 2 beats, bar 2= 2 beats, bar 3 = 3 beats, bar 4 = 5 beats.
   - The time signature for bar 4 is 5/4, because there are 5 crotchets (quarter notes) in total.

2. If you can divide the bar into 3 equal beats:
   - Work out the total value of **one beat**. If the total value is a dotted note, the time signature will be compound. Otherwise, it will be simple time.
   - In **simple** time the lower number 2=minim (half note) 4=crotchet (quarter note) and 8=quaver (8th note).
   The top number will be 3.
   - In **compound** time the lower number 4=dotted minim (dotted half), and 8=dotted crotchet (dotted quarter).
   The top number will be 9.

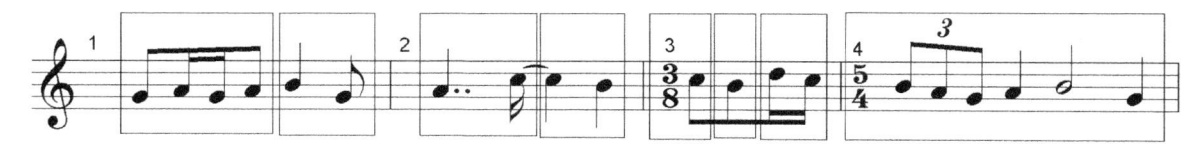

   - In bar 3, one beat equals one quaver (8th note), so the time signature is 3/8.

3. If you can divide the bar into 2, now try to divide it again, into 4. Remember that in quadruple time, we must normally be able to see the **3rd beat** of the bar clearly. If the 3rd beat of the bar is not obvious, then it is probably duple time. (See below for some exceptions). Remember that ties are useful because they show where new beats start. Decide if the bar is duple or quadruple. Sometimes both are possible.

4. Work out the total value of one beat. As before, if the total value is a dotted note, the time signature will be compound. Otherwise, it will be simple time.
    - In **simple** time: lower number 2=minim (half note) 4=crotchet (quarter note) and 8=quaver (8th note).
      The top number will be 2 for duple time, or 4 for quadruple.
    - In **compound** time: lower number 4=dotted minim (dotted half), and 8=dotted crotchet (dotted quarter). (ABRSM: Dotted quaver (dotted 8th) = 16).
      The top number will be 6 for duple time, or 12 for quadruple.
    - Bar 1 cannot be divided into 4. Remember that in compound time, notes are always grouped into **single** beats, so we would not see the semiquavers (16ths) joined together if one beat is equal to a dotted quaver (dotted 8th), because the group would total **two** beats. This must be duple time. One beat = dotted crotchet (dotter quarter), so the time signature is 6/8.

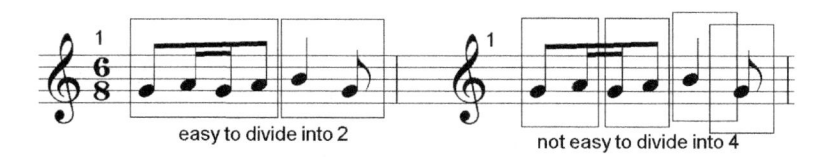

      easy to divide into 2   not easy to divide into 4

    - If bar 1 was correctly notated for quadruple time, it would look like this. (12/16 is not tested at Trinity Grade 5, but may come up in ABRSM Grade 5).

    - In bar 3 it is not particularly easy to divide the first box into 2, but it is easy to divide the end of the bar, and the 3rd beat of the bar is clearly shown by the tie. This could be duple or quadruple.

Exceptions

In quadruple time the 3rd beat of the bar is not "obvious" in the following rhythms:

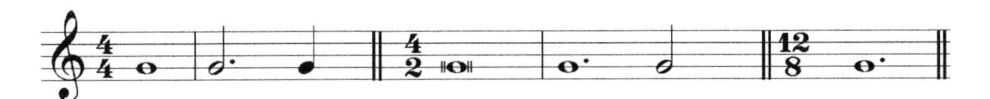

41

4/4 or 2/2?

There is no difference between 4/4 and 2/2 in the way the notes are **written**. There is a difference in how a conductor would indicate the beats: in 4/4 the conductor will indicate four in a bar, and in 2/2 she will indicate two in a bar. In a fast tempo, this helps the conductor to wave her arms about less!

There are two archaic time signatures which are still used today for 4/4 and 2/2. These are just an older method and there is no difference between C and 4/4 in the way they are played, or conducted.

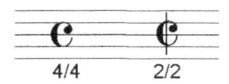

Rewriting a Melody in a New Time Signature

In this type of question, you are asked to rewrite a short excerpt using a different time signature **without changing the rhythmic effect.**

This is easy if both the old and new time signatures are simple time.

Notice how the note values change when **3/4** becomes **3/8**:

Each note value is halved; for example, a minim becomes a crotchet and a dotted minim becomes a dotted crotchet (half note becomes a quarter note and dotted half note becomes a dotted quarter note).

Compound to Simple (and Vice Versa)

The task is more complicated when you are moving from simple time to compound time or vice versa, and when you also have to work out what the new time signature is!

The first step is to look at the given time signature and remind yourself **what kind** of beat and **how many** beats it represents.

Let's take 12/8 as an example.

12/8 = 4 **dotted crotchet** (dotted quarter note) beats per bar.

The equivalent **simple** time signature will use the same value of note **without the dot**. Which time signature uses four **undotted** crotchets (quarter notes) per bar? 4/4.

Each **dotted main beat** in compound time should be written as an **undotted** note in simple time:

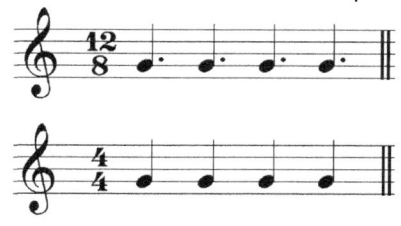

In simple time, when the beat is split into two halves, we simply write two notes worth half a beat each. To achieve the same thing in compound time, we must use a duplet. The actual note values used (quavers (8th notes)) here, stays the same – just add a "2" symbol.

In simple time, when the beat is split into thirds, we have to use a triplet symbol. To achieve the same thing in compound time, we only need to remove the triplet sign and copy the notes as they are.

Here is a rhythm in 9/8. How would you rewrite it in a simple time signature? Try to answer the questions, then check on the next page.

1. How many beats and how long is each beat, in 9/8?
2. What is the equivalent **simple** time signature?
3. The first note F is a dotted crotchet (dotted quarter note). What should this be in the new time signature?
4. The second main beat is a crotchet + quaver (quarter + eighth note). How should this be written in the new time signature?

The third main beat is the same rhythm as the second main beat (minus the tie). Rewrite the whole rhythm:

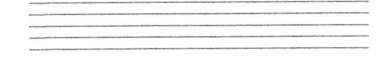

1. 9/8 is compound triple time. It means there are three dotted crotchets (dotted quarter notes) per bar.
2. The equivalent simple time signature is 3/4, with three undotted crotchets (quarter notes) per bar.
3. A dotted crotchet (dotted quarter) will become an undotted crotchet (quarter note) in the new time signature.
4. In 9/8, a crotchet (quarter note) is worth 2/3 of the beat, and a quaver (eighth note) is worth 1/3. To make the same rhythm in simple time, you need to use a triplet symbol, to divide up the beat into three instead of two. The note values remain the same – just add a triplet sign.

Here is the whole bar rewritten:

Common Mistakes In Rewriting Time Signatures

The most common mistake I find among students tackling this question, is failing to work out what the **new** time signature is supposed to be. Often, a student will assume that a bar in 6/8 ought to be rewritten in 3/4, because they contain the same number of quavers (eighth notes) per bar. This is a mistake! 6/8 is duple time, and 3/4 is triple time, so it is impossible to rewrite a rhythm in that way without **changing the rhythmic effect**. Always keep the same number of main beats per bar: duple time **stays** as duple time, and so on.

Rests sometimes make the exercise look more difficult, but you should think about them in exactly the same way as you think about notes.

A common mistake, (especially with compound times), is to forget that a rest sometimes makes up a whole beat with the note **before** it.

In this bar, the 9/8 time signature might make you think that you should group quavers into threes, so you might think the second beat of the bar starts with the quaver (eighth) rest:

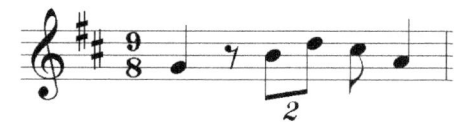

Look more closely, and you'll see that the first complete beat, (which must be a dotted crotchet (dotted quarter note) beat), is the G **plus** the rest. The second beat is the duplet B - D, and the third beat is C sharp - A.

Rests can be included in duplets and triplets in the same way that notes can. Here's an example:

GROUPING OF NOTES BY BEATS

This list shows the regular time signatures. The first bar shows the main beats only. Bar 2 shows how the main beats are subdivided. Bar 3 shows how the subdivisions are further divided. The main beat can be divided into two (simple time) or three (compound time), but the second subdivision is always into two. Notice how the beaming reflects the number of main beats per bar. When notes are beamed in sixes, they always represent **three** higher level beats (not two). In 2/4 it is also correct to beam all 4 quavers (8th notes) together.

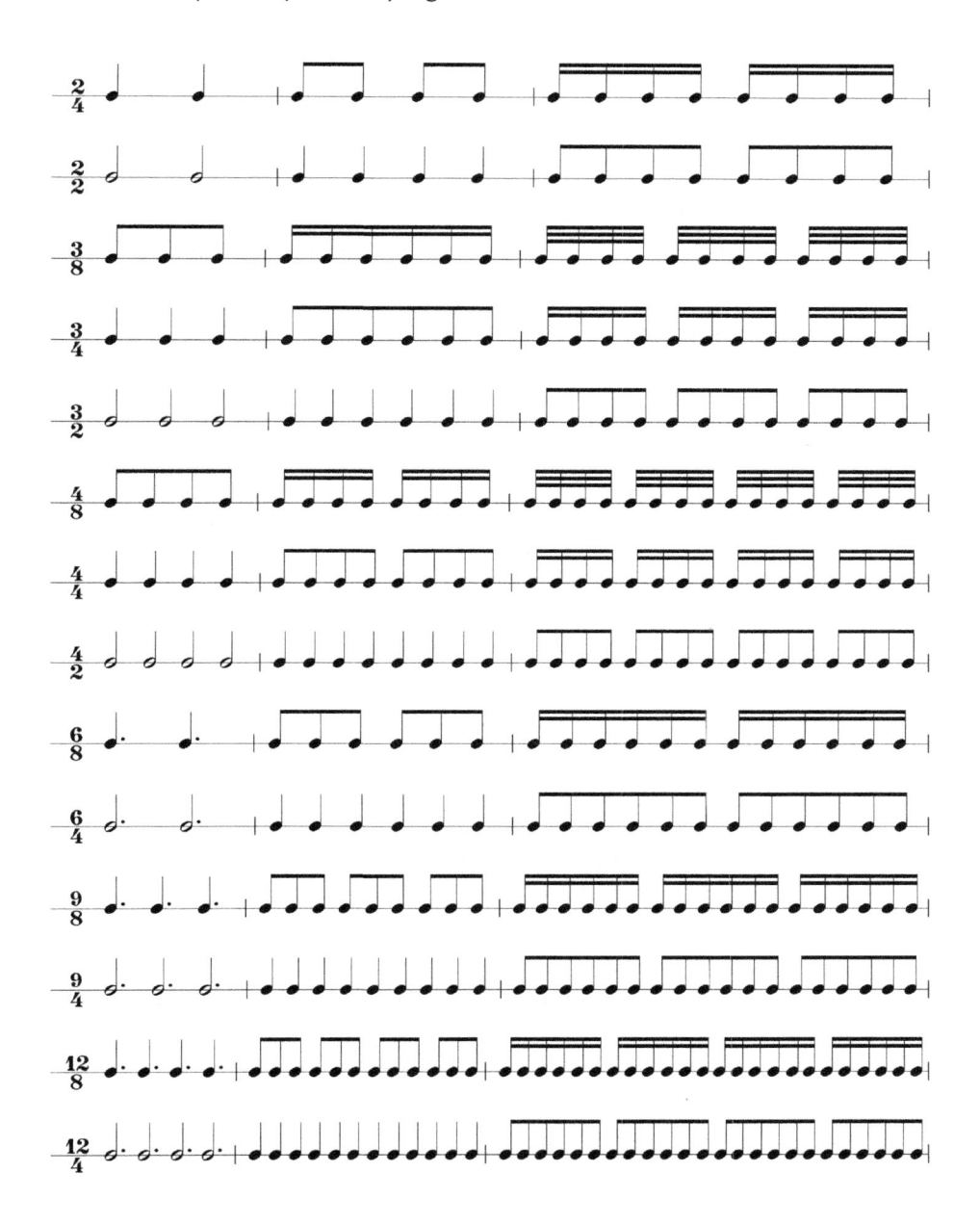

TIME SIGNATURE EXERCISES

Exercise 1: Time Signatures - Technical Names

Describe each of these time signatures as:

- Simple or compound AND
- Duple, triple or quadruple

Or, as irregular.

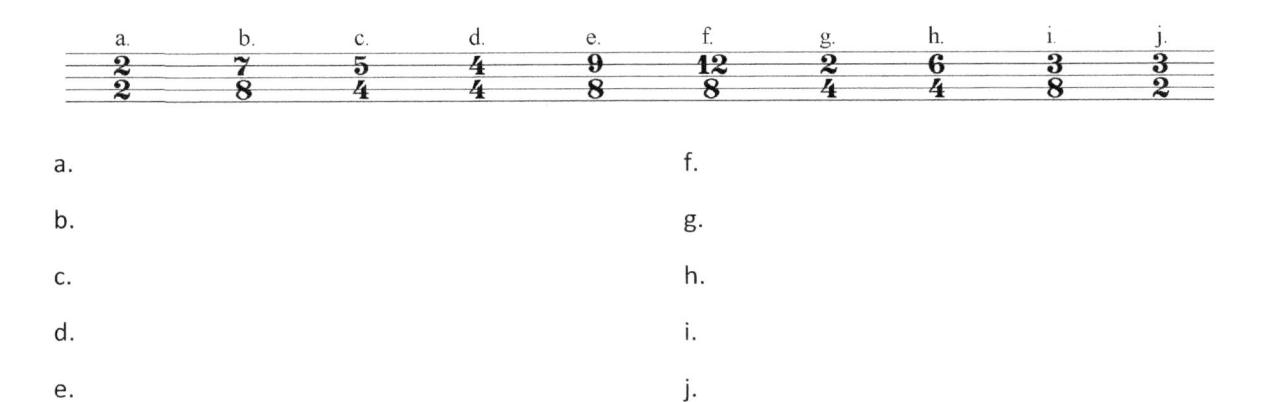

a. 2/2   b. 7/8   c. 5/4   d. 4/4   e. 9/8   f. 12/8   g. 2/4   h. 6/4   i. 3/8   j. 3/2

a.

b.

c.

d.

e.

f.

g.

h.

i.

j.

Exercise 2: Time Signatures - Meanings

3/2 represents **3 minim (half note) beats** per bar. What do the following time signatures represent?

a. 4/2   b. 12/4   c. 6/8   d. 9/4   e. 3/4   f. 11/8   g. 3/8   h. 5/8   i. 7/4   j. 4/8

a.

b.

c.

d.

e.

f.

g.

h.

i.

j.

Exercise 3 - Adding Bar Lines

Put the missing bar lines in the following passages, which all begin on the first beat of the bar:

a.

b.

c.

d.

Exercise 4 - Understanding Time Signatures

a. Which two **simple** time signatures can have a lower number 8?

b. When there are two tied notes, which one must fall on a new main beat: the first note or the second?

c. How can you tell the difference between 3/2 and 6/4?

d. In compound time, is the main beat a dotted or undotted note?

e. In which type of time signature does the main beat divide up into two: simple or compound?

Exercise 5 - Adding Time Signatures

Add the correct time signatures to each of these bars.

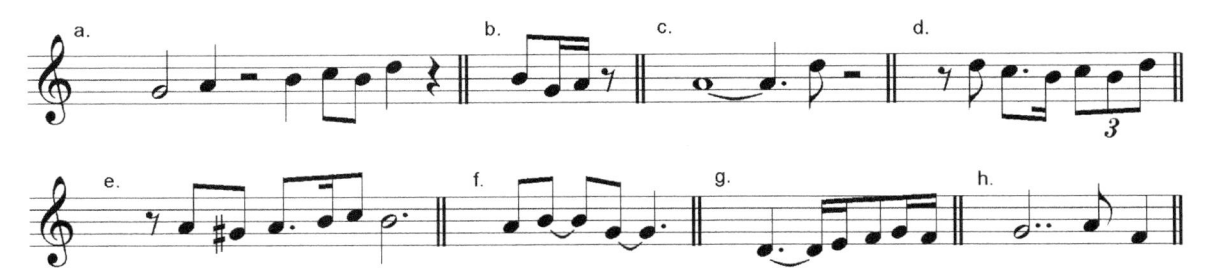

Exercise 6 - Rewriting a Rhythm without Changing the Rhythmic Effect

For each of the following simple time melodies;

    a. Describe the time signature as duple/triple/quadruple

    b. Convert the time signature to **compound time**

    c. Write in the new time signature and rewrite the rhythm without changing the rhythmic effect.

For each of the following compound time melodies;

    a. Describe the time signature as duple/triple/quadruple

    b. Convert the time signature to **simple time**

    c. Write in the new time signature and rewrite the rhythm without changing the rhythmic effect.

TIME SIGNATURES ANSWERS

Exercise 1

a. Simple duple

b. Irregular

c. Irregular

d. Simple quadruple

e. Compound triple

f. Compound quadruple

g. Simple duple

h. Compound duple

i. Simple triple

j. Simple triple

Exercise 2

a. Four minims (half notes)

b. Four dotted minims (dotted half notes)

c. Two dotted crotchets (dotted quarter notes)

d. Three dotted minims (dotted half notes)

e. Three crotchets (quarter notes)

f. Eleven quavers (eighth notes)

g. Three quavers (eighth notes)

h. Five quavers (eighth notes)

i. Seven crotchets (quarter notes)

j. Four quavers (eighth notes)

Exercise 3

Exercise 4

a. 3/8 and 4/8

b. The second

c. 3/2 has three minim (half note) beats per bar, whereas 6/4 has two dotted minim (dotted half note) beats per bar

d. Dotted

e. Simple

Exercise 5

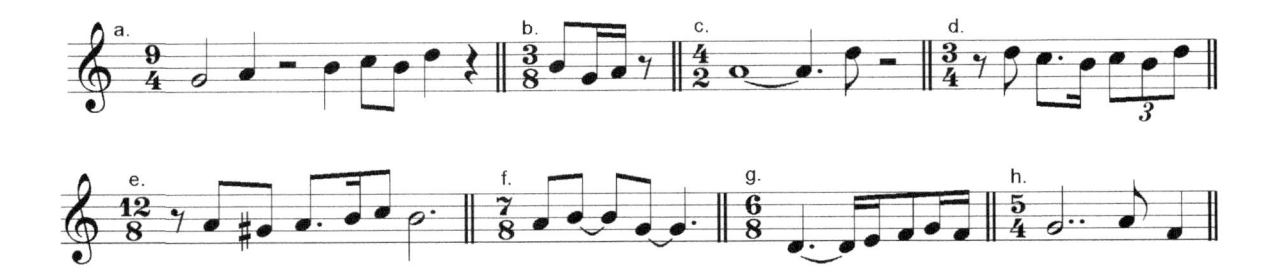

Exercise 6

Duple time

Triple time

Duple time

Quadruple time

4. CLEFS

THE TWO MAIN CLEFS

The most frequently used clefs are **treble clef** and **bass clef**.

The treble clef is also called the 'G' clef, because it curls around the line of music where we find G (**above** middle C):

In the same way, the bass clef encircles the line where we find F (**below** middle C), so it's also called the 'F' clef:

Historically, these symbols started out as the actual letters 'G' and 'F', but became more stylised over time. Make sure you can draw them correctly!

THE STAVE, AND THE GRAND STAFF

When we write music on a single group of 5 lines, this group is referred to as a stave (or staff).

Sometimes we need to use two (or more) **staves,** because the range of an instrument is particularly wide, (for example, the piano or harp.) The staves are connected together on the left-hand side by a bracket, like so:

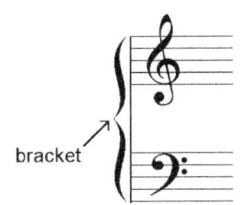

This is also known as the **grand staff**. The grand staff usually uses the treble clef and the bass clef.

Octave Clefs

A small "8" hanging below a clef is used to show that the music actually sounds an **octave** lower than indicated.

1: C **above** middle C
2: Middle C

3: Middle C
4: C **below** middle C

This clef is most often seen in a tenor voice part.

Alto and Tenor Clefs (or "C" Clefs)

Smaller instruments, which play notes mainly above middle C, only use the treble clef. These include the violin, flute, clarinet, oboe and trumpet.

But some bigger, lower-pitched instruments, like the bassoon, trombone or cello, have a range which is partly above and partly below middle C. If we only used the treble or bass clefs for these instruments, we would end up using a lot of ledger lines:

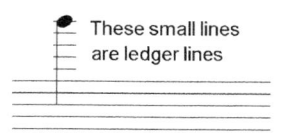

These small lines are ledger lines

Ledger lines are quite difficult to read, so the **clef is changed to suit the pitch** of the music.

These bigger instruments use 'C' clefs: clefs which tell the player where **middle C** is, (as well as bass clef and treble clef where necessary).

There are two main 'C' clefs, both of which you need know for Grade 5 Theory:

Alto clef – **third** line is middle C

Tenor clef – **fourth** line from bottom is middle C

As you can see, the alto and tenor clefs are the **same** shape. This is because they are both 'C' clefs - they tell you which line middle **C** is found on.

The pointed central part of the C clef tells you where middle C lies. If you look carefully, you'll see that the tenor clef sits a little higher up than the alto clef.

When you know where middle C is, you can work out where the other notes are.

Look at two chromatic scales using alto and tenor clefs:

Alto clef:

E F F# G G# A A# B C C# D D# E

Tenor clef:

C Db D Eb E F F# G Ab A Bb B C

WHICH INSTRUMENTS USE THE ALTO CLEF?

These days, the only instrument which uses the alto clef is the **viola**.

Sometimes it is called the "viola clef" for this reason.

(Historically, it was used in vocal music, by the oboe and by other instruments.)

WHICH INSTRUMENTS USE THE TENOR CLEF?

The bassoon, cello and trombone all use the tenor clef. The tenor voice does **not** use the tenor clef.

GRADE 5 QUESTIONS

In ABRSM Grade 5 Theory, you need to be able to **transpose** music between any of the clefs.
Normally you have to keep the pitch **exactly** the same (but read the question carefully!)

Usually, you're only asked to transpose about one bar into a new clef.

You might be asked questions about the clefs which certain instruments use.

Transposing to a New Clef

Usually, you'll have to transpose from a common clef (treble or bass) to a less common C clef, but you should be prepared for anything.

Follow these steps, and you should succeed every time.

In this piece, which is for flute (top stave) and piano (lower two staves), your task is to transpose the left hand piano part in bars 3 and 4 into the tenor clef, without changing the pitch. The bars you need to transpose are marked with a bracket.

First, double check the current clef (1). This is the bass clef.

Next, look at the first note you have to transpose (2) and work out whether it is **above or below middle C**.

This note is Bb **below middle C.**

Now look at the new clef and remind yourself where **middle** C is located - it is marked on the line here:

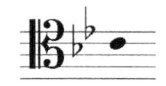

Our first note is one step lower than middle C, so write it in on the space below, then continue with the rest of the notes, including any accidentals if necessary.

You will probably have to change the stem directions on some notes - be careful! Notes which are above the middle line have stems pointing down, and vice versa. Notes on the middle line are correct in either position. In these two bars, we had to change the stem direction on the third note, F. The last note, A, is on the middle line, so the stem can go either way.

You don't need to work out every note name. Count lines and spaces only, e.g. next space down, two lines up etc.

Key signatures in the alto and tenor clefs are covered in the next lesson.

CLEFS EXERCISES

Exercise 1 - Drawing Clefs

Draw the following clefs as carefully as you can:

Bass clef Alto clef Treble clef Tenor clef

Exercise 2 - Clefs and Instruments

Which clef(s) do these instruments normally use?

1. Flute
2. Oboe
3. Clarinet
4. Bassoon
5. Trumpet
6. Trombone
7. Violin
8. Viola
9. Cello

Exercise 3 - Reading Clefs

Write the note names under each note in the following extracts.

(Don't forget to check the key signature, and to write the note names in capital letters!)

a.

b.

c.

d.

Exercise 4 - Rewriting in a New Clef

Rewrite the following bars marked **x,** using the clefs provided.

a.

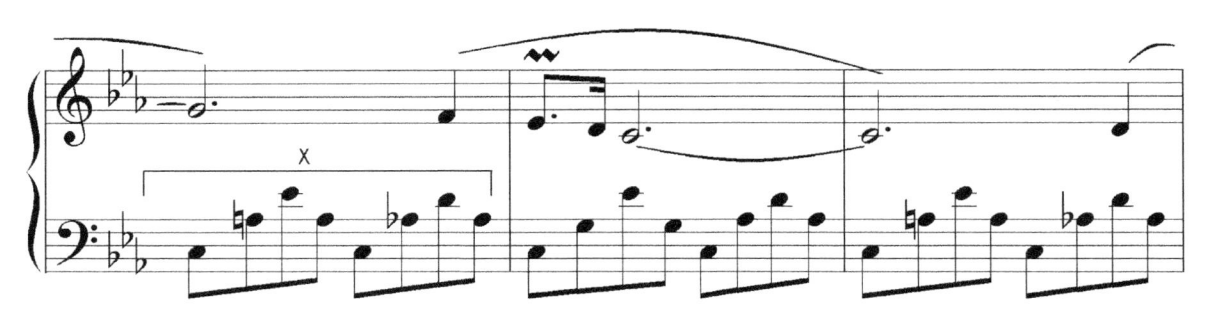

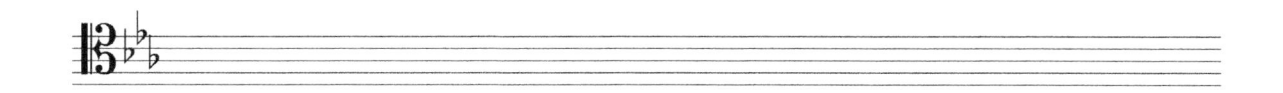

b.

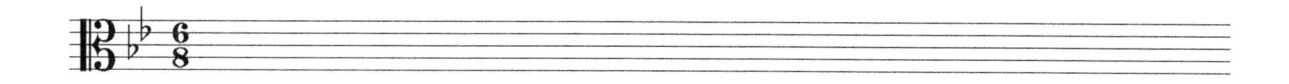

56

CLEFS ANSWERS

Exercise 1

Bass clef   Alto clef   Treble clef   Tenor clef

Exercise 2

1. Treble clef
2. Treble clef
3. Treble clef
4. Treble, bass and tenor clefs
5. Treble clef
6. Treble, bass and tenor clefs
7. Treble clef
8. Alto clef
9. Treble, bass and tenor clefs

Exercise 3

a.

C E G C B A G Bb A G F Ab

b.

B A G D Eb C B D F# G Ab

c.

B C# D F# G# A F# B

d.

G F# G A Bb Eb D C D F# A Eb D

Exercise 4

a.   b.

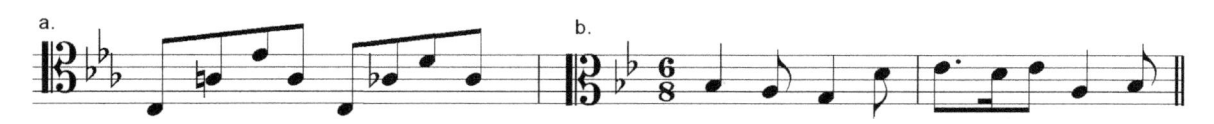

57

5. KEY SIGNATURES
What are key signatures and why do they exist?

(See also the mymusictheory.com video on Key Signatures
https://www.youtube.com/watch?v=u7vhkl_DMlg).

In your ABRSM Grade 5 Theory exam, all the musical examples are based on **tonal** music. Every piece of tonal music is in a certain **key,** which will be either major or minor.

The key signature tells you what that key is. Key signatures are used in order to make it unnecessary to fill up the staves with flats and sharps on many notes. Also, without a key signature, you would have to do some detective work to find out what key a piece is actually in.

Each key signature represents **two** keys: one minor key and one major key. Here are some examples, with the keys they represent:

| G Major | Bb Major | Eb Major |
| E Minor | G Minor | C Minor |

| E Major | B major | Gb Major |
| C# Minor | G# Minor | Eb minor |

How do I write a key signature?

You must write key signatures very carefully. There are two important things to remember about writing them:

- The position on the stave
- The order of the sharps or flats

You will need to know how to write **any** key signature up to six sharps/flats in **any** clef for Grade 5 Theory!

The **sharps** are written in this order: F#, C#, G#, D#, A#, E#.

G major - F#;

D major - F#, C#;

A major - F#, C#, G#;

E major - F#, C#, G#, D#;

B major - F#, C#, G#, D#, A#;

F sharp major - F#, C#, G#, D#, A#, E#

in these positions on the stave (Treble, Bass, Alto then Tenor clef):

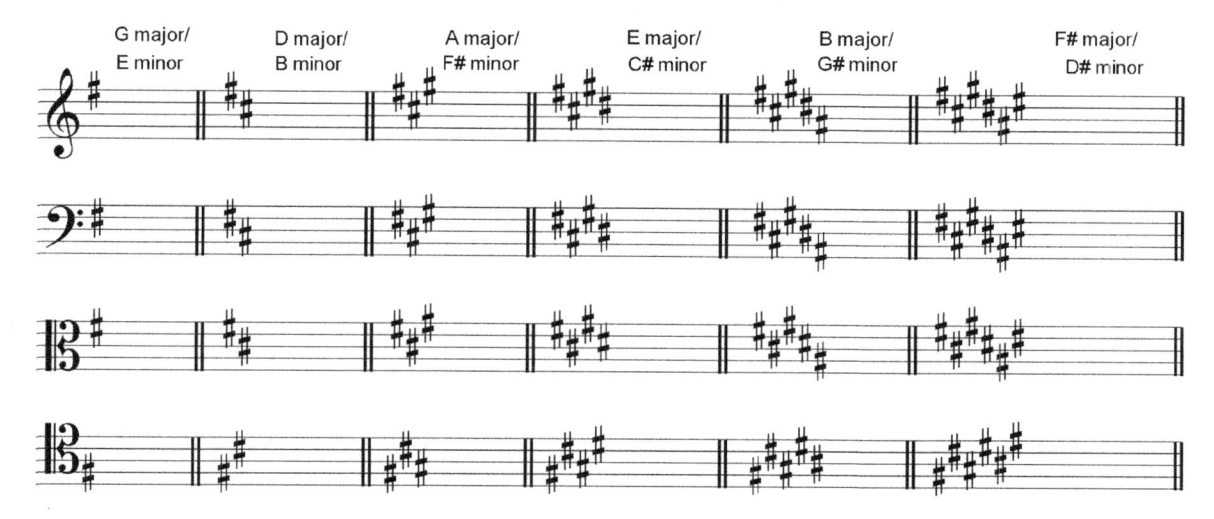

The **flats** are written in this order: Bb, Eb, Ab, Db, Gb, Cb

F major - Bb;

Bb major - Bb, Eb;

Eb major - Bb, Eb, Ab;

Ab major - Bb, Eb, Ab, Db;

Db major - Bb, Eb, Ab, Db, Gb;

Gb major - Bb, Eb, Ab, Db, Gb, Cb;

in these positions:

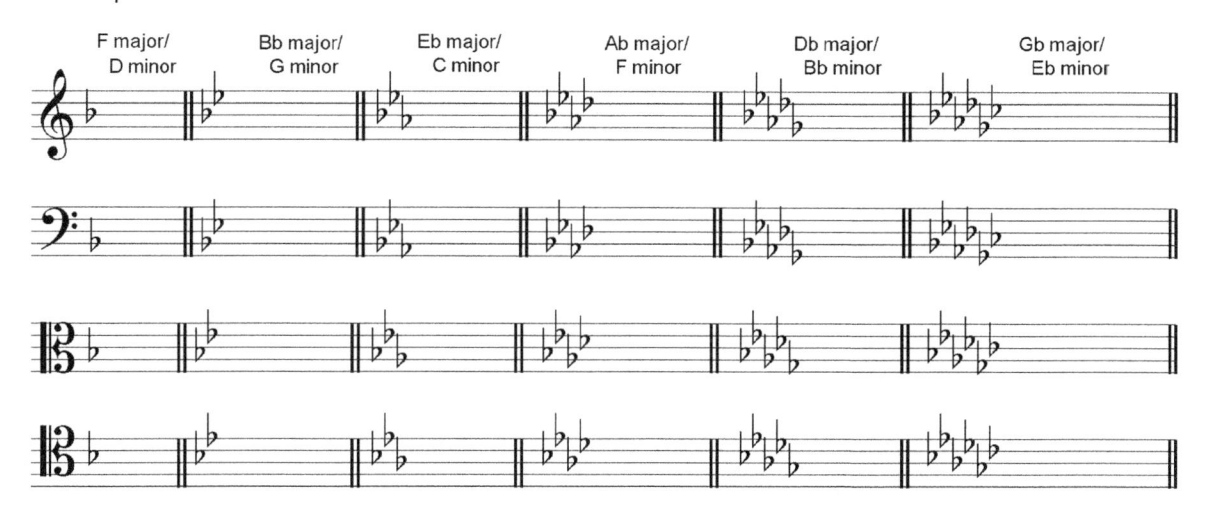

How can I learn all these different key signatures?

1. Position on the Stave

Learning how to write key signatures correctly isn't as hard as you might think.

With the sharp keys, the general "up-down" pattern is the same for treble, bass and alto clef. However, **tenor** clef is quite different and has to be learnt separately.

With the flat keys, **all** the clefs follow the same basic "up-down" pattern. Try to memorise the patterns.

Look again at the examples above, and notice where the pattern is the same and where it is different.

Make sure you never write a sharp/flat on a ledger line in a key signature!

2. Order of Flats and Sharps

To remember the order of the sharps, start at F (#) and then count **5** notes forward: F-G-A-B- **C**. The next sharp is **C#**. Repeat the process to find the next sharp: C-D-E-F- **G**, so the next sharp is **G#**, and so on.

To remember the order of the flats, starting at B(b), count **4** notes forward: B-C-D- **E**, so the next flat is **Eb**. Repeat the process to find the next flat: E- F- G- **A**, so the next flat is **Ab**, and so on.

Remember that you count **5** for sharps- the word "sharp" has **5** letters!

Remember that you count **4** for flats- the word "flat" has **4** letters!

Another method is to learn a phrase like this:

Father - **C**hristmas - **G**ave - **D**addy - **A**n - **E**mpty - **B**ox

The first letter of each word gives you the order of sharps. F-C-G-D-A-E-B. Write the letters backwards to find the order of flats B-E-A-D-G-C-F! (This phrase has seven sharps and flats, but you only need to learn up to six for grade 5 theory!)

How do I work out a major key from a key signature?

Sharps

If you have a sharp key signature, look at the **last sharp** in the pattern. This is the **leading note,** which is the 7th note in the scale. The next semitone up will be the **tonic**, or 1st note in the scale, and will be the major key. For example, look at the following key signature:
The **last sharp** in the pattern is G#. The next semitone up is A, so this key signature represents A Major.

Flats

If you have a flat key signature, you'll first have to remember that F major uses 1 flat (Bb). For all key signatures with 2 or more flats, the **last but one** flat in the pattern represents the major key.
For example, look at the following key signature:
The **last but one** flat in the pattern is **Db**, so this key signature represents **Db** major.

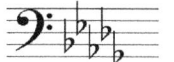

How do I work out a minor key from a key signature?

The minor key represented by a key signature is always that of the 6th note of the scale in the major key (also called the sub-mediant). For example, in C major, which has no flats or sharps, the 6th note is **A**:

So, **A minor** also has no flats or sharps. We say that A minor is the "relative minor" of C major.

Use the same method for flat and sharp key signatures:

A major => F# minor

Ab major => F minor

How to Work Out the Key of a Piece of Music

You might be asked what key a piece of music begins in, or **modulates** (changes key) to. The simplest way to do this is usually to look at the notes which are being used, and then see what major or minor harmonic **scale** they belong to. For example, if a piece of music has two sharps in the key signature and includes A#s, it's probably in B minor (because there are A#s in the B minor harmonic scale). This method isn't fool-proof however.

The only fool-proof method involves looking at the harmony, so we'll talk about this more in lesson 10, on **Chords**.

KEY SIGNATURES EXERCISES

Exercise 1

State the major and minor keys represented by the following key signatures:

a. (bass clef, 1 sharp)

b. (bass clef, 3 flats)

c. (treble clef, 7 sharps)

d. (alto clef, 2 sharps)

e. (alto clef, 4 flats)

f. (treble clef, 2 flats)

g. (bass clef, 2 sharps)

h. (alto clef, 4 flats)

Exercise 2

Write the key signatures which represent the following keys, using the clefs provided.

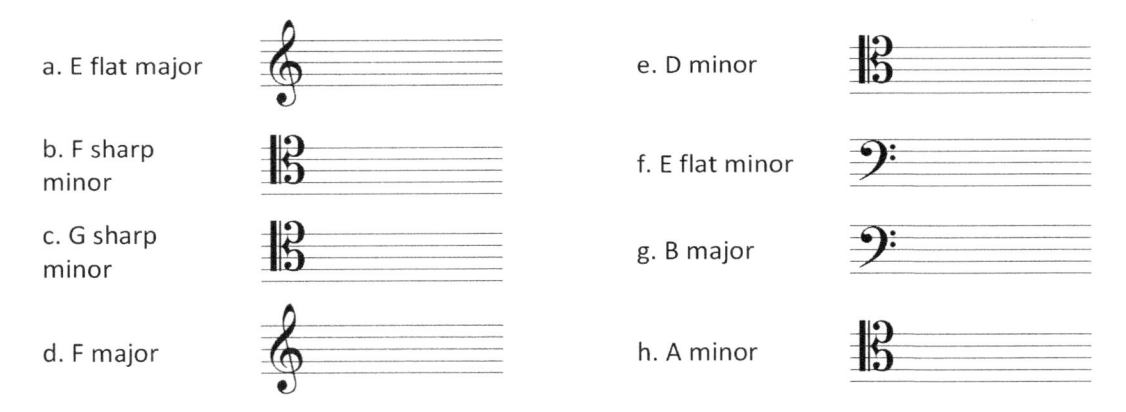

a. E flat major (treble clef)

b. F sharp minor (alto clef)

c. G sharp minor (alto clef)

d. F major (treble clef)

e. D minor (alto clef)

f. E flat minor (bass clef)

g. B major (bass clef)

h. A minor (alto clef)

Exercise 3

a. Which two keys have 6 flats in the key signature?

b. Which two keys have 4 sharps in the key signature?

c. Which two keys have 3 flats in the key signature?

KEY SIGNATURES ANSWERS

Exercise 1

a. G major/E minor

b. Ab major/F minor

c. F# major/D# minor

d. A major/F# minor

e. Db major/Bb minor

f. Bb major/G minor

g. D major/B minor

h. Gb major/Eb minor

Exercise 2

a. E flat major

b. F sharp minor

c. G sharp minor

d. F major

e. D minor

f. E flat minor

g. B major

h. A minor

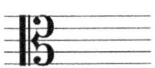

Exercise 3

a. Gb major and Eb minor

b. E major and C# minor

c. Eb major and C minor

6. SCALES

A scale is a series of notes going up (ascending) or down (descending). For Grade 5 Music Theory, you need to know about **diatonic** scales and **chromatic** scales.

Diatonic Scales

A diatonic scale has 7 different notes and each of those notes is given **different** letter name, A-G.

There are 3 main types: **major**, **minor harmonic**, and **minor melodic**. (There is also another type of minor - "natural minor", but you won't be tested on this).

Diatonic scales are usually played and written in groups of 8 notes, so that they sound finished. The 8th note is the same as the 1st note, but an octave higher or lower.

So,

A, B, C, D, E, F, G#, A[1] is a correct scale, but

A, B, C, D, E, F, Ab, A natural is **not** a correct scale, because the **letter name A** has been used twice: once as "A flat" and once as "A natural". (Even though you might think that G# and Ab are the same note, they aren't!)

We talk about diatonic scales as being in a certain key, for example, in "C Major". Most of the scales you will have played up to now will have been diatonic scales. They are the most common type of scale in Western classical music.

You need to know how to write all the major, minor harmonic and minor melodic scales, with up to **six sharps or flats** in the key signature. You are asked to write scales starting on the tonic, which is the technical name for the first note of the scale.

Tones and Semitones

All scales have something in common; they have a defined pattern of **tones** and **semitones**.

Imagine a piano keyboard: two neighbouring keys (whatever colour) are **semitones** (also known as "half steps").
E to F is a semitone. A to B flat is one too, and so is G to G sharp.
If you take two notes with one note between them, you'll have found a **tone** (also known as a "whole step").
C to D is a tone, as are C# to D sharp , E to F# and G to A.

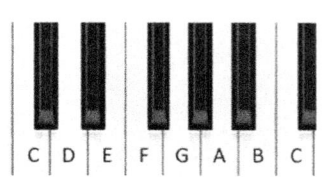

64

MAJOR SCALES

All major scales are made up with the following pattern, where T=tone and S=semitone:

T – T – S – T – T – T – S

Here are two examples:

G Major

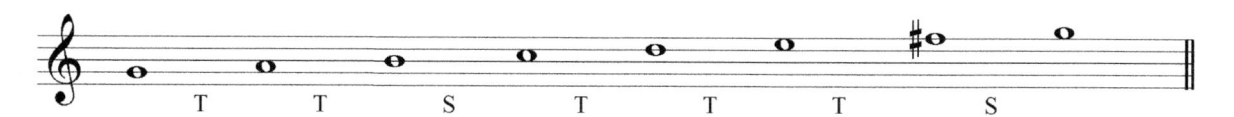

G to A is a tone, A to B is a tone, B to C is a semitone, and so on.

F# Major

F# to G# is a tone, G# to A# is a tone, A# to B is a semitone, and so on.

If you've ever wondered why we need notes like "E sharp" when "F" seems to be the same note, you'll see that we need them in keys like F sharp major! (Remember, you can only use each letter name once per octave).

If you write a major scale **with** a key signature, there are **no** accidentals to add.

Minor Harmonic Scales

All minor harmonic scales have the following pattern, where **3S**=three semitones:

T – S – T – T – S - **3S** – S

For example:

D Minor Harmonic

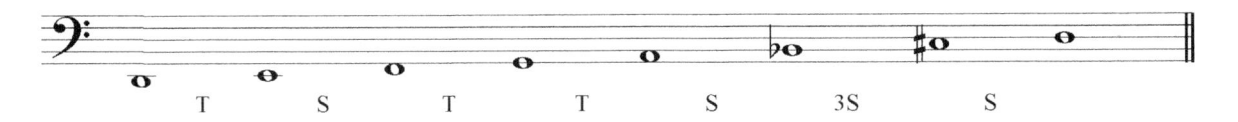

Bb to C# is three semitones.

F Minor Harmonic

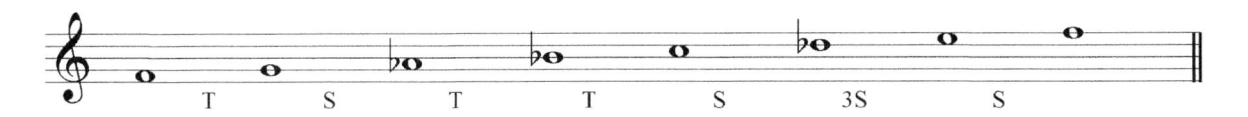

Db to E natural is three semitones.

Minor harmonic scales use the **same** notes on the way down, in reverse order.

If you write a harmonic scale **with** a key signature, you always have to add **one** accidental, which will **raise** the note by **one semitone.**

In an ascending scale it is the 7th note, in a descending scale it is the 2nd. It could be a natural, sharp or double sharp sign, but it's **never** a flat sign.

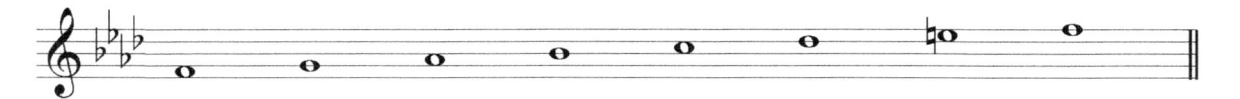

Here is F minor harmonic written with a key signature. The key signature includes Eb, so we raise the 7th note by a semitone to **E natural**.

Minor Melodic Scales

Minor melodic scales are a little more difficult, because they have one pattern on the way up and a **different** pattern on the way down:

Minor melodic ascending: **T – S – T – T – T – T – S**

Minor melodic descending: **T – T – S – T – T – S – T**

For example, here are the ascending and descending scales of C melodic minor:

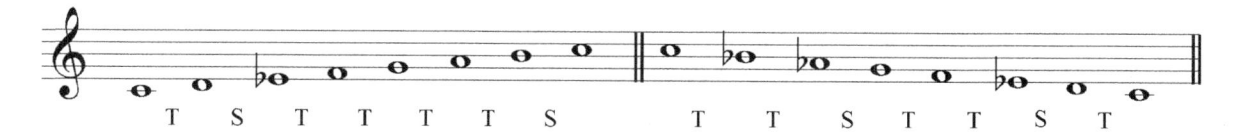

T S T T T T S   T T S T T S T

Notice that on the way up we have A natural and B natural, but on the way down we have A flat and B flat: the descending scale is **different** from the ascending one.

If you write an **ascending** melodic minor scale **with** a key signature, you always have to add **two** accidentals, (natural, sharp or double sharp signs), to the 6th and 7th notes, to **raise** each one by a **semitone**. Here is C minor melodic ascending, with the 6th and 7th degrees of the scale **raised by a semitone**.

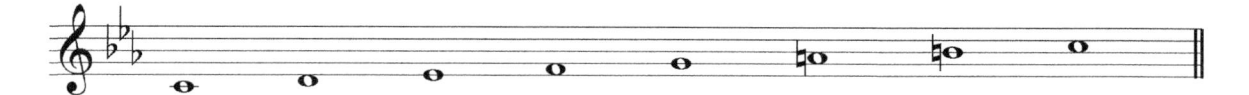

If you write a **descending** melodic scale with a key signature, there are **no** accidentals to add. Here is C minor melodic descending.

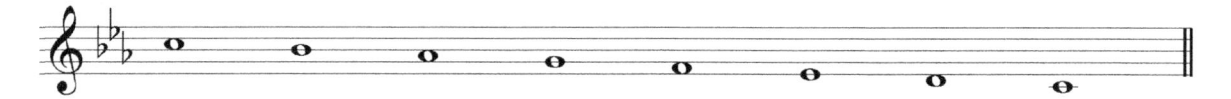

Technical Names

We use "technical" names to talk about each note of the diatonic scale, instead of saying "first note", "third note" and so on. You need to learn these technical names because there are often general knowledge questions about them in Grade 5 Theory!

1st note: Tonic

2nd note: Supertonic

3rd note: Mediant

4th note: Subdominant

5th note: Dominant

6th note: Submediant

7th note: Leading note

Technical names are worked out from **ascending** scales.

For example, in C major ascending, the second note we write is D, so D is the supertonic in C major.

(If we write out the scale of C major **descending**, the second note we write is B. But B is **not** the supertonic. The supertonic is still D; B is the leading note, because it is the 7th note in the **ascending** scale.)

CHROMATIC SCALES

A chromatic scale has 12 notes, and each step of the scale is a semitone.

If you start on a C and play every available note until you arrive at the next C, you have played a chromatic scale. We don't talk about chromatic scales as being "in" a particular key; we just talk about the note they start "on" - and they can start on any note.

Here is an ascending chromatic scale starting on C:

You need to be able to recognise chromatic scales and might have to find a section of a chromatic scale within a piece of music, or write out a chromatic scale.

To find a section of a chromatic scale, look for a series of notes that are all **one semitone** apart. There will have to be **accidentals** included somewhere – so scan the page for accidentals first, to find possible locations! If you write a chromatic scale, make sure the first and last notes are the same type, and don't use the same letter name three times (e.g. Cb-C-C#).

HOW TO WRITE DIATONIC SCALES

First, read the instructions very carefully, and underline the **keywords** about whether the scale should be:

- **ascending or descending**
- **major, minor harmonic or minor melodic**, or **chromatic**
- whether you should use a **key signature** or not.

Next, pay attention to the **clef**! (All this may sound obvious, but many students lose points when writing scales simply because they mis-read the question!)

Here's an example question:

> Using semibreves (whole notes), write one octave of the ascending G# harmonic minor scale. ***Do not use a key signature***, but add any necessary accidentals.

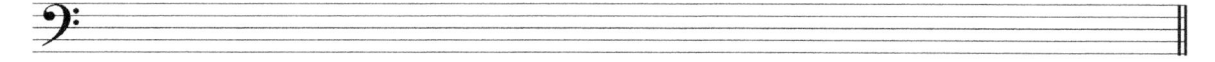

First, write in eight notes, starting with the tonic and finishing on another tonic. You can write the accidental on to the tonics (top and bottom) but don't add any other accidentals yet. Make sure that you write only **one** note per letter name: **one note on each line and space**.

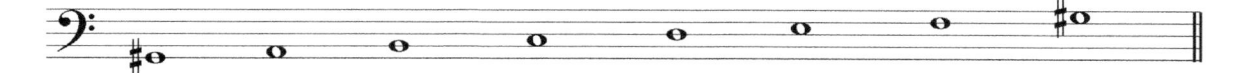

Next, using the pattern for ascending harmonic minor scales (**T – S – T – T – S – 3S – S**), add the necessary accidentals. You can sketch a piano keyboard out if it helps.

For example, the first step is a tone, so we add a sharp to the A, to get G#-A#. The next step is a semitone, and A#-B is already a semitone, so there is nothing to add to the B. Continue for the rest of the scale.

Notice that we needed an F## (double sharp) on the 7th note. F## is an enharmonic equivalent of G natural, but G natural would not be correct here, since we already use the letter name G for the tonic note.

Here's another question.

> *Write one octave of the descending F minor harmonic scale using semibreves (whole notes). Use a key signature and add any other necessary accidentals.*

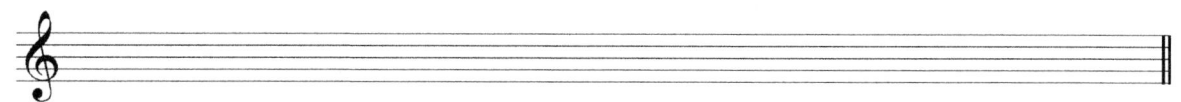

This time, we need to add a key signature, so that is the first thing to put in. The key signature for F minor has four flats. (See Lesson 5 on Key Signatures).

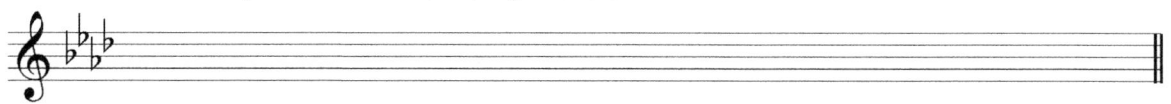

Next, write out eight notes from F to F, using each letter name once. Look again at the scale **direction** before you start: this will be a **descending** scale.

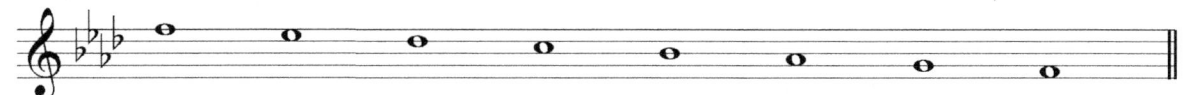

Finally, add any necessary **accidentals**. When you use a key signature, you only ever need to add accidentals to

- a minor harmonic scale, or
- an **ascending** minor melodic scale.

This is F minor **harmonic**, so we need to raise the 7th degree of the scale by a semitone.

Remember that the 7th degree of the scale is based on the **ascending** scale, so it is the note E in this case (count up 7 notes from the bottom F). Next, look again at the **key signature**: does it affect this note? In this case, yes it does. The 7th degree of the scale is actually **E flat**. We need to raise this by a semitone, so it will become **E natural**. Put in the accidental, and the scale is finished.

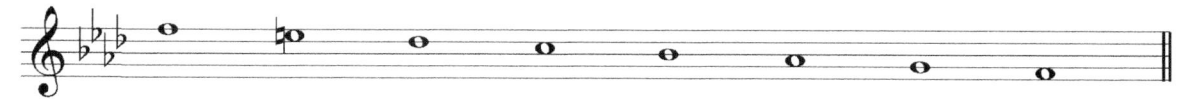

Don't forget, an ascending **melodic** minor scale will need both the 6th and 7th degrees raising by a semitone.

COMMON ERRORS

If you're learning an instrument, you've probably played all these scales already, but you might have learnt to play them without thinking about the actual notes, (your fingers do the thinking!)

In Grade 5 Theory, you might be asked to write any scale, ascending or descending, either with a key signature or using accidentals. Here are some common *mistakes*: make sure you don't make them!

- Not noticing a **bass clef**.
- Not using a **different** letter name for each note.
- Not noticing whether the question asks for a **key signature** or **accidentals**.
- Writing accidentals/key signatures on the **wrong space** or **line.**
- Writing an **ascending** scale when the question asks for a **descending** one, and vice versa. (Remember "**D**" for "**D**own" and "**D**escending").
- Writing a **harmonic** instead of a **melodic** scale, or vice versa.
- Using the wrong note value - usually you are asked to use **semibreves**.
- Forgetting to add an accidental to the last note of a scale, if necessary. Remember, an accidental on the first note of the scale (e.g. Bb) will NOT affect the same note an octave higher!
- Forgetting to add naturals in a chromatic scale, if the previous note was flattened. For example, this chromatic scale is wrong:

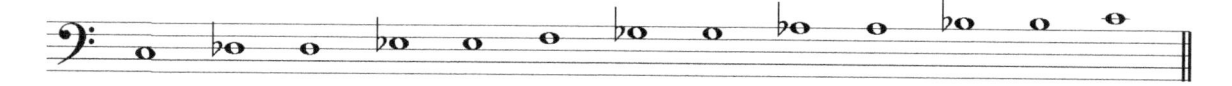

After a flat has been written, it affects any further notes of the same pitch, so this scale actually begins C-Db-Db-Eb-Eb! The correct way to write it is this:

SCALES IN ALL FOUR CLEFS

You may be asked to identify the correct clef of a scale. The correct clef might be treble, bass, alto or tenor.

Here are some facts about scales which might help you to find the answer quickly:

- The tonic (keynote) will never be E#, Fb, A#, B# or Cb.
- Only two scales combine both flats and sharps: they are **D minor** (harmonic, and ascending melodic) and **G minor** (harmonic, and ascending melodic). (There are no major scales which use both flats and sharps).
- All scales (major and minor) contain the following intervals above the tonic (keynote):
    - Tonic-supertonic = major 2nd
    - Tonic-subdominant = perfect 4th
    - Tonic-dominant = perfect 5th
- All minor scales have a minor 3rd above the tonic.
- All major scales have a major 3rd above the tonic.

(Intervals are covered in detail in the next chapter).

Here's an example question:

Select the correct clef to form a **minor scale:**

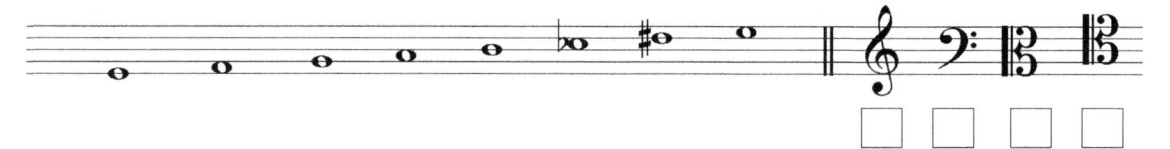

In this scale, there is one sharp, and one flat. This means we can narrow it down to either D minor or G minor. If you know your scales well, you might quickly see that it must be D minor, because the flat and sharp in the scale are **adjacent** notes (Bb and C#, 6th and 7th degrees of the scale). In G minor (melodic) the flat and sharp and Bb and F#, which are the 3rd and 7th degrees of the scale.

If you are less confident about spotting scale shapes, you will need to use a bit of trial and error, to check which scale works. Try each clef in turn, using your knowledge of intervals above the tonic:

- With a treble clef, the tonic would be E, so this can't be the right clef, because it must be D or G.
- With a bass clef, the first note would be G, but the third note would be B (natural), so it can't be a minor scale in the bass clef.
- With an alto clef, the tonic would be F, so this can't be the right clef.
- A process of elimination tells us that it must be tenor clef, but you can also check that in tenor clef the first note is D, the third is F (minor 3rd above tonic), the 4th is G (perfect 4th above tonic) and the 5th is A (perfect 5th above tonic).

Here's another example. Which clef will make this into a minor scale?

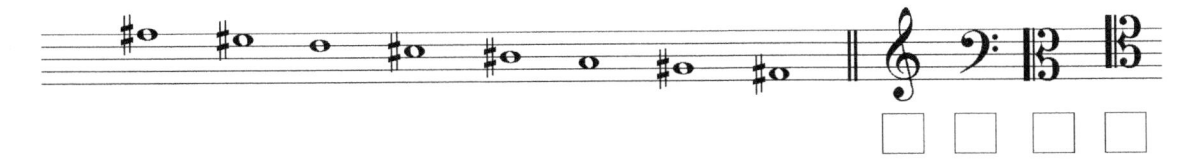

This time there are only sharps, and it's a descending scale, so we can't narrow it down so easily as in the previous example.

The best way to begin is by working out the tonic for each clef, then looking at the intervals above the tonic. As this is a descending scale, we need to work backwards, from the lower tonic.

- In the treble clef, the lowest note (tonic) is F#.
    - Minor 3rd above tonic ✓ (A)
    - Perfect 4th above tonic X (B#)
    - Cannot be treble clef

- In the bass clef, the tonic is A#.
    - A# isn't used as a tonic, so cannot be bass clef

- In the alto clef, the tonic is G#.
    - Minor 3rd above tonic ✓ (B)
    - Perfect 4th above tonic ✓ (C#)
    - Perfect 5th above tonic ✓ (D#)
    - Seems correct, but let's check tenor clef too.

- In the tenor clef, the tonic is E#.
    - E# isn't used as a tonic, so cannot be tenor clef.

SCALES EXERCISES
Exercise 1 - Mistakes in Scales

Correct the **mistakes** in the following scales. There could be one or two mistakes in each scale.

a. D melodic minor ascending

b. F melodic minor descending

c. F sharp harmonic minor descending

d. G flat major descending

e. A flat major ascending

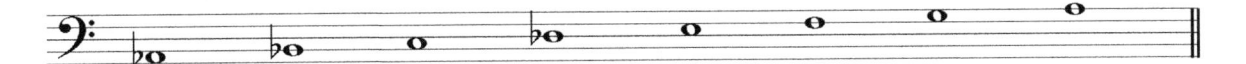

Exercise 2.1 - Ascending Scales with Key Signatures

Write one **ascending** octave of the major, minor harmonic and minor melodic scales that have these key signatures, (add any necessary accidentals). Use semibreves (whole notes) and start on the tonic. Name the key of each scale.

a.
Major

Minor harmonic

Minor melodic

b.
Major

Minor harmonic

Minor melodic

c.
Major

Minor harmonic

Minor melodic

74

Exercise 2.2 - Descending Scales with Key Signatures

Write one **descending** octave of the major, minor harmonic and minor melodic scales that have these key signatures, (add any necessary accidentals). Use semibreves (whole notes) and start on the tonic. Name the key of each scale.

a.
Major

Minor harmonic

Minor melodic

b.
Major

Minor harmonic

Minor melodic

c.
Major

Minor harmonic

Minor melodic

EXERCISE 3.1 - ASCENDING SCALES WITH ACCIDENTALS

Write one octave **ascending** of each of the following scales. Do **not** use a key signature but put in all the necessary sharp or flat signs. Use semibreves (whole notes) and begin on the tonic.

a. D flat major

b. C melodic minor

c. E major

d. E flat major

e. A melodic minor

f. C sharp harmonic minor

Exercise 3.2 - Descending Scales with Accidentals

Write one octave **descending** of each of the following scales. Do **not** use a key signature but put in all the necessary sharp or flat signs. Use semibreves (whole notes) and begin on the tonic.

a. B flat harmonic minor

b. D major

c. C sharp melodic minor

d. B melodic minor

e. A major

f. E flat harmonic minor

EXERCISE 4 - FINDING CHROMATIC SCALES IN A MELODY

Look at this extract for piano. Draw a bracket

- over four successive notes in the right-hand part that form part of a chromatic scale, and
- over five successive notes in the left hand that form part of a chromatic scale.

EXERCISE 5 – WRITING CHROMATIC SCALES

a. Using semibreves (whole notes) write one octave of the ascending chromatic scale beginning on Db.

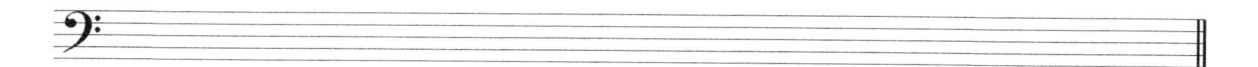

b. Add accidentals to this scale, to make a chromatic scale beginning on F#.

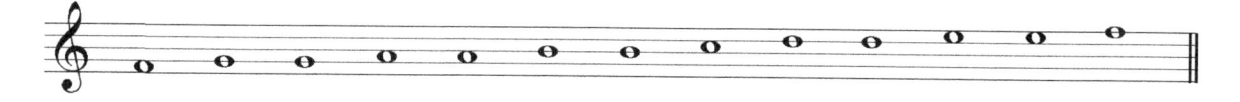

EXERCISE 6

a. Which clef (treble, bass, alto or tenor) would make this a **major** scale?

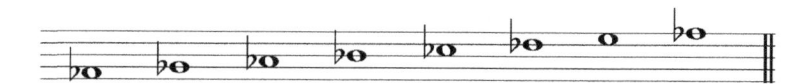

b. Which clef (treble, bass, alto or tenor) would make this a **minor** scale?

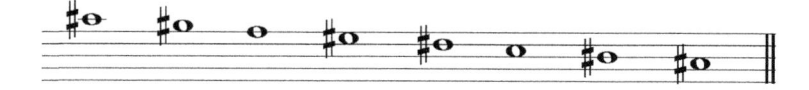

c. Which clef (treble, bass, alto or tenor) would make this a **minor** scale?

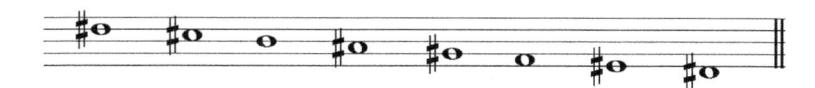

d. Which clef (treble, bass, alto or tenor) would make this a **major** scale?

SCALES ANSWERS
Exercise 1

X marks the errors

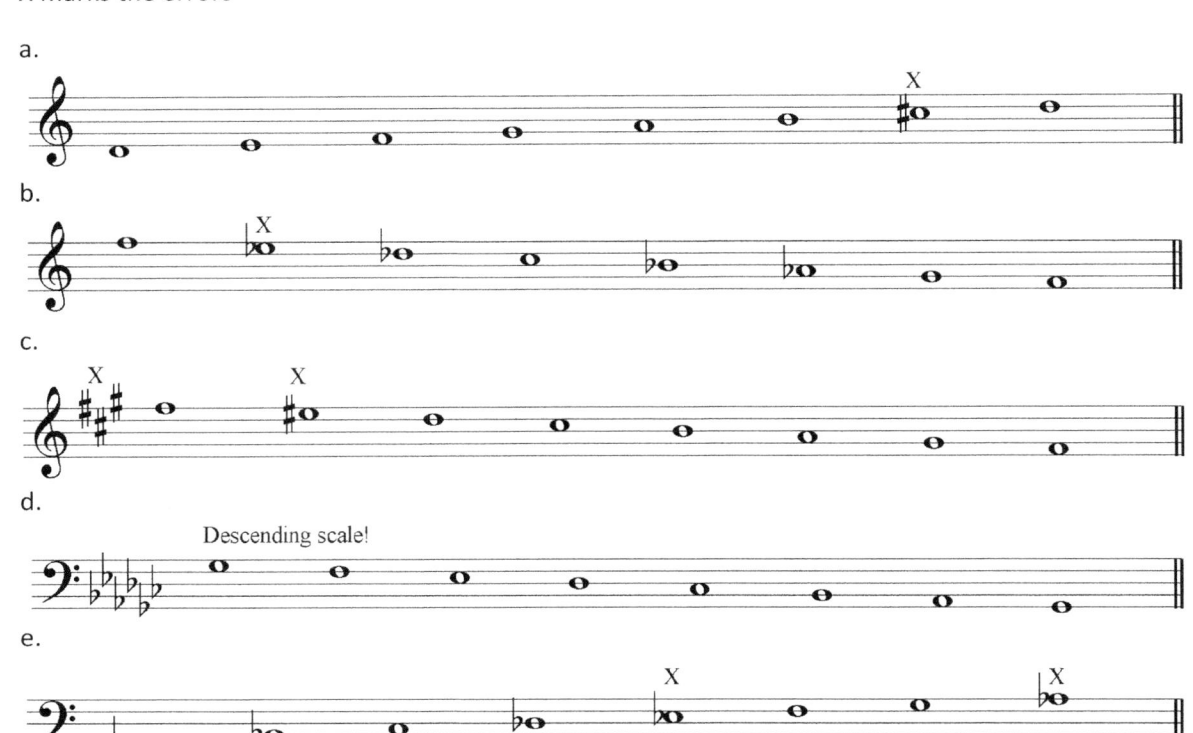

a.

b.

c.

d. Descending scale!

e.

Exercise 2.1

a. Major — G major; Minor Harmonic — E minor; Minor Melodic

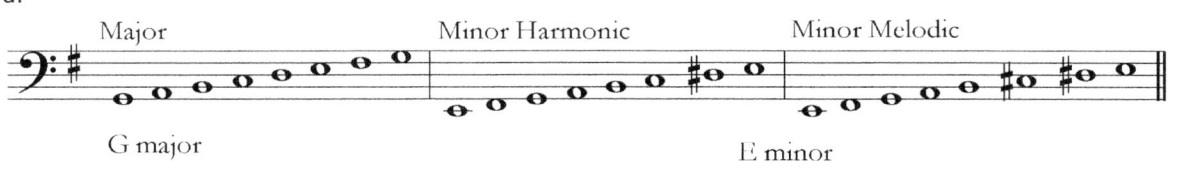

b. Major — A flat major; Minor Harmonic — F minor; Minor Melodic

c. Major — F sharp major; Minor Harmonic — D sharp minor; Minor Melodic

EXERCISE 2.2

a.

Major — Minor Harmonic — Minor Melodic

Bb major — G minor

b.

Major — Minor Harmonic — Minor Melodic

F major — D minor

c.

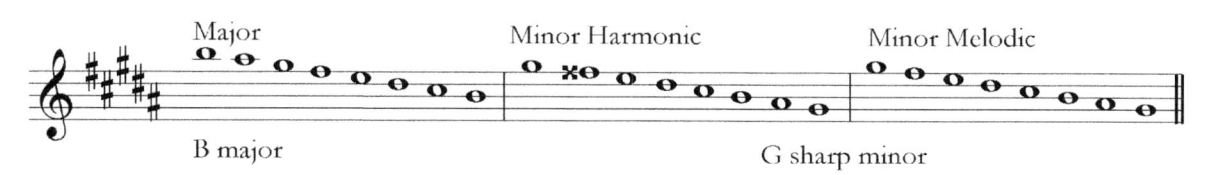

Major — Minor Harmonic — Minor Melodic

B major — G sharp minor

EXERCISE 3.1

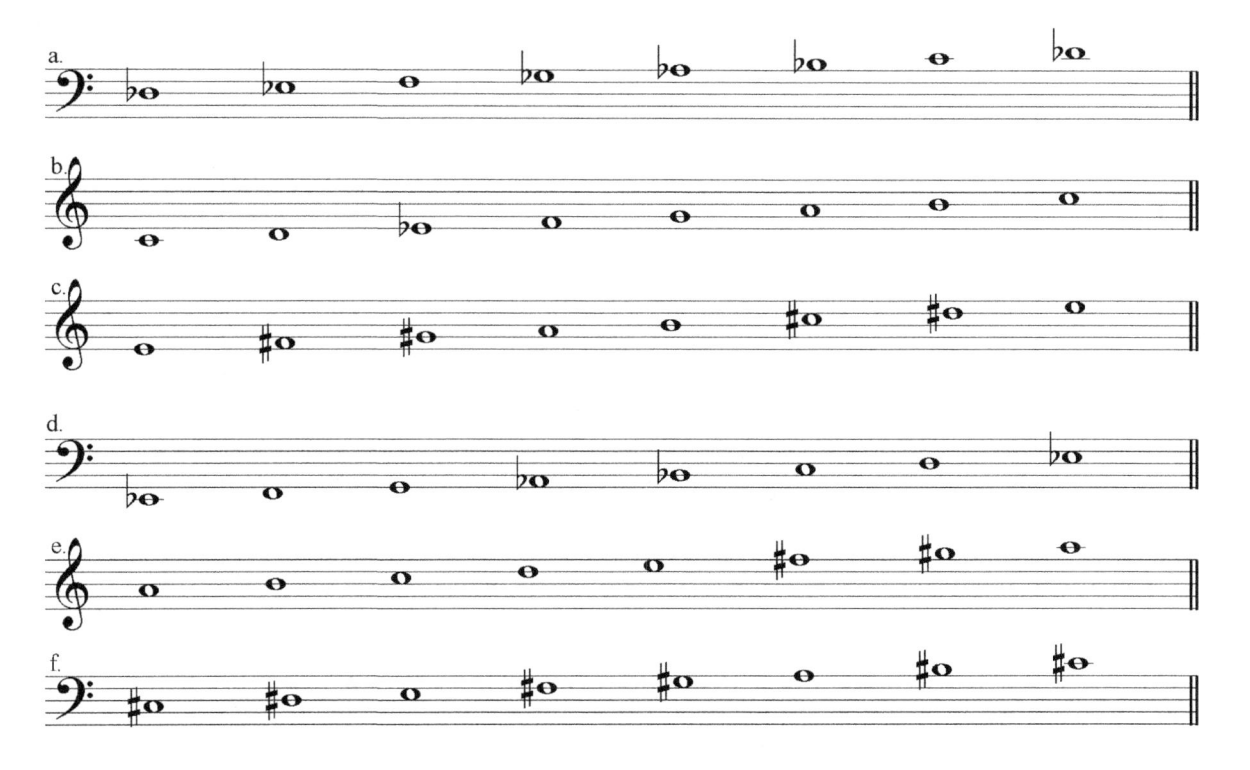

a.

b.

c.

d.

e.

f.

81

EXERCISE 3.2

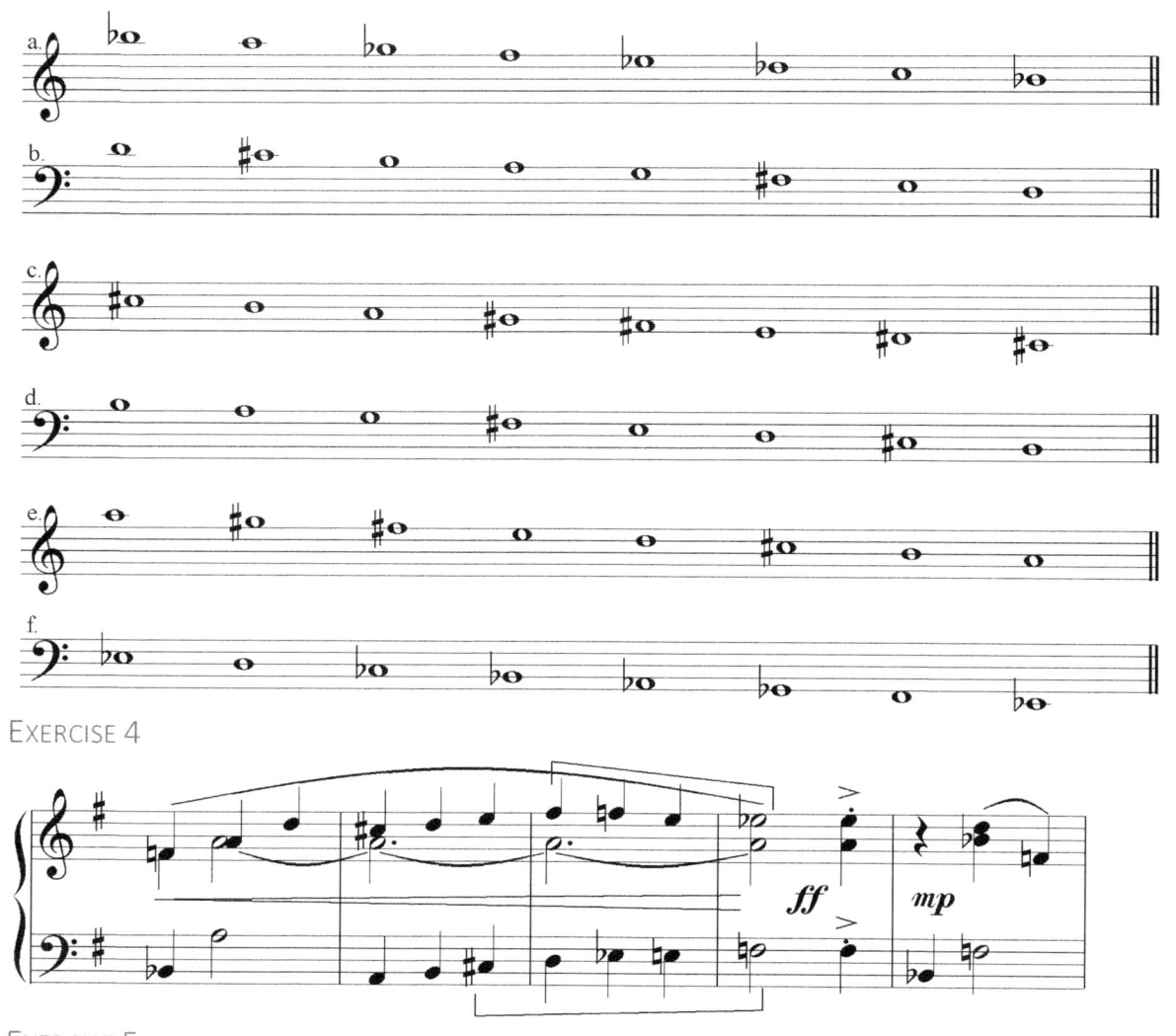

EXERCISE 4

EXERCISE 5

a. There are several ways to write this correctly. Make sure that the first and last notes are both D flat (with an accidental), that the same letter name has not been used three times, and that any necessary naturals have been added.

b.

EXERCISE 6

a. Alto (Gb major) b. Bass (G# minor melodic) c. Tenor (C# minor harmonic) d. Alto (Bb major)

7. INTERVALS

You might also like to watch the MyMusicTheory video lesson on intervals at https://www.youtube.com/watch?v=7vIb8MO3H8k

WHAT ARE INTERVALS?

An "interval" is the distance between any two notes. Each interval has a **number** and a **quality**, which you have to know for Grade 5 Music Theory.

"Melodic intervals" are read horizontally and are found in melodies, whereas "harmonic intervals" are read vertically, and are found in chords.

They are described in the same way.

B-D as a melodic (horizontal) interval and as a harmonic (vertical) interval.

INTERVAL NUMBERS

To find the number of an interval, first find the letter names of the two notes, (ignore any sharps and flats for now), and count the letter names, starting with the **lower note on the stave.**

If the letter name is the same, the interval will be either **"unison"** (the same note), or **"octave"** (the next one up or down the stave). The other intervals use the ordinal numbers "2nd", "3rd" and so on.

In the above intervals, the interval number is a **3rd**, because there are three letter names B-C-D.

STARTING ON THE HIGHER NOTE - A VERY COMMON MISTAKE!

What happens if you try to calculate an interval by starting with the higher note on the stave? You will get the wrong answer! This is a common mistake, so let's look at an example of what can go wrong. What is the following melodic interval?

First, the correct way: starting on the **lower** note (C), we count letter names to the higher note, (G), C-D-E-F-G =5, which gives us a 5th. This is the right answer!

Now the wrong way. Starting on the **first note** (G), we count the letter names to the second note (C), G-A-B-C =4, which gives us a 4th. This is the wrong answer!

Some examples:

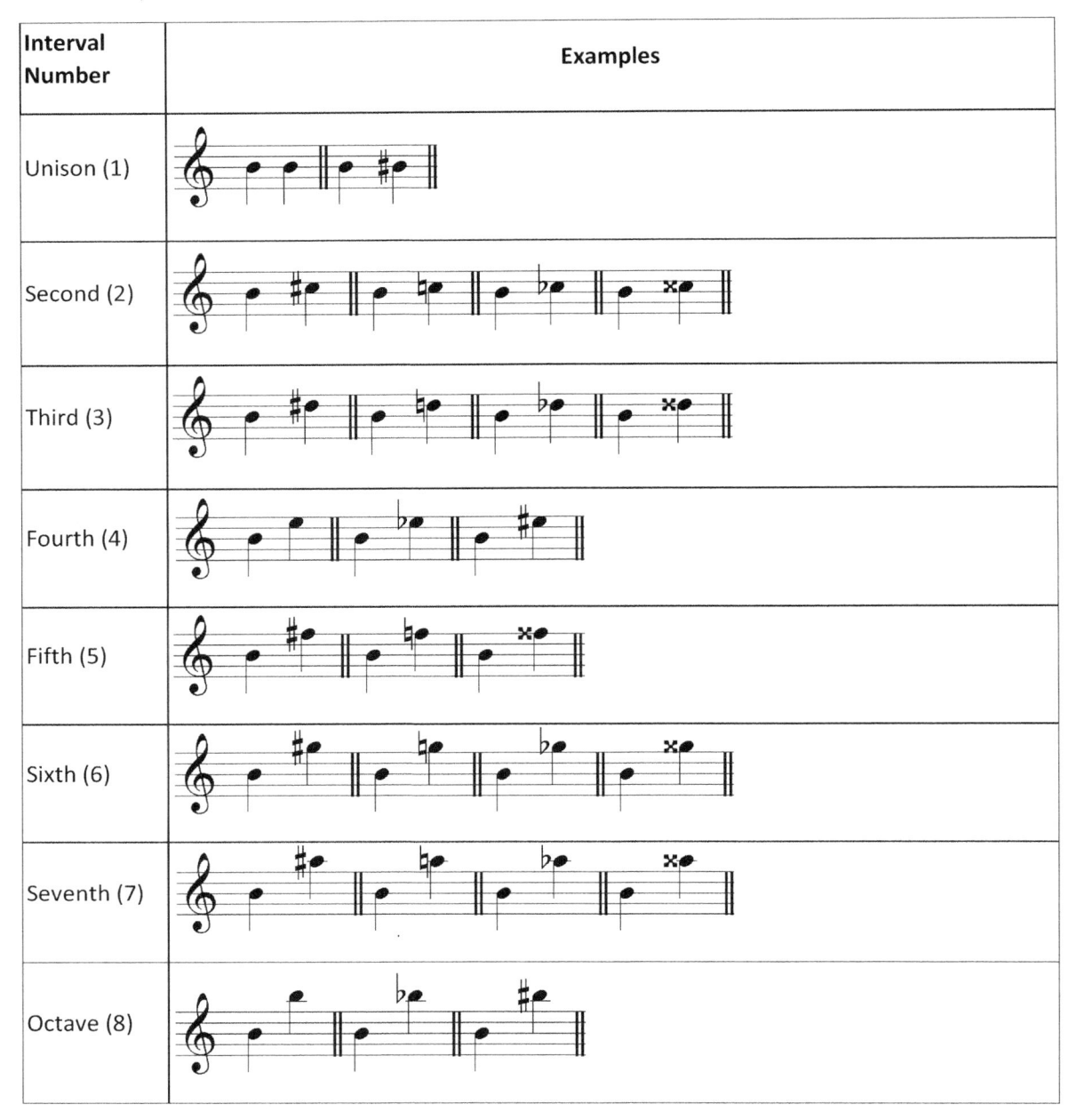

Interval Number	Examples
Unison (1)	
Second (2)	
Third (3)	
Fourth (4)	
Fifth (5)	
Sixth (6)	
Seventh (7)	
Octave (8)	

INTERVAL QUALITIES

Each interval has quality name which goes before it, for example "**major** sixth".

There are 5 quality names which are: **perfect, major, minor, augmented** and **diminished**.

We will look at each of these interval qualities in more detail.

MAJOR AND PERFECT INTERVALS

If you take a **major scale**, all the intervals which are built from the **tonic** of that scale are either **major** or **perfect**. You can think of "major and perfect" as the kind of "default intervals". Here's an example. Look at the scale of G major, where G is the tonic (keynote).

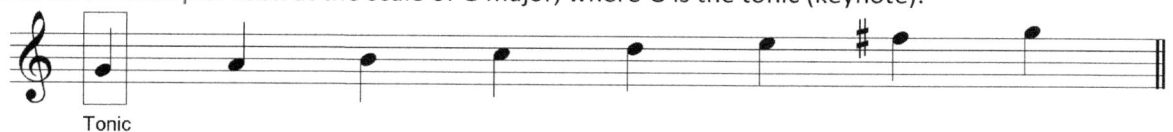

Tonic

If the lower note of an interval is G, and the upper note is one which exists in the G major scale, its quality will be either **major** or **perfect**.

Major intervals are the 2nd, 3rd, 6th and 7th, and **perfect** intervals are the unison, 4th, 5th and octave. (Notice that there are four of each kind).

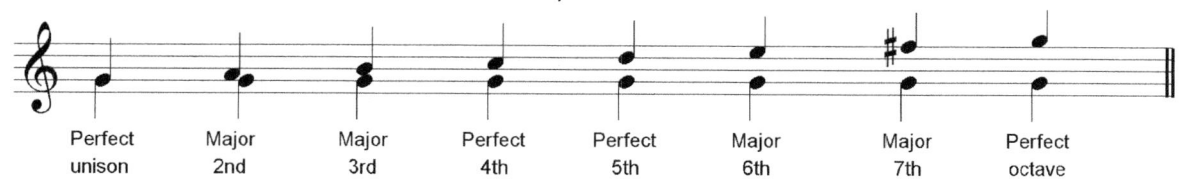

Perfect unison | Major 2nd | Major 3rd | Perfect 4th | Perfect 5th | Major 6th | Major 7th | Perfect octave

The same is true of any major scale. So, in order to understand intervals, it is essential that you are confident in your scales!

If the upper note in an interval is **not** part of the major scale built from the lower note, then the interval cannot be major or perfect. Instead, it will be **augmented, minor or diminished**.

AUGMENTED INTERVALS

When an interval is **wider by one semitone** than the one found in the major scale, then the interval is **augmented**.

Here's an example:

First, work out the interval number: count up the letter names (ignore any accidentals). G-A-B-C-D = 5 notes = a 5th. Next look at the 5th in the G major scale: the note is D natural.

In this interval, we have D sharp instead. The D# means that this interval is one semitone wider than the one found in the major scale. Therefore, this interval is an **augmented 5th**.

In fact, if you raise **each note** of the major scale by a semitone (**without changing the letter names of the notes**[1]), you will make all the intervals augmented:

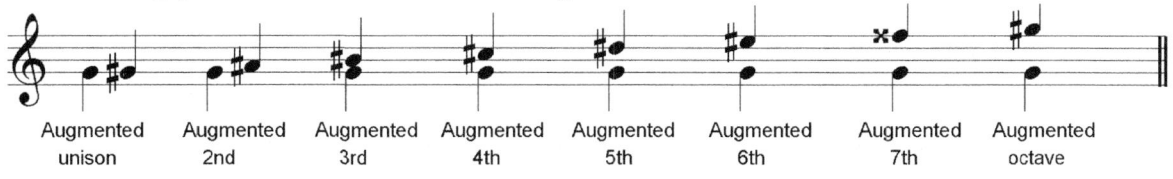

Augmented unison | Augmented 2nd | Augmented 3rd | Augmented 4th | Augmented 5th | Augmented 6th | Augmented 7th | Augmented octave

Notice that in order to raise the F# by a semitone, we need to use a double sharp.

---

[1] i.e. you should change G to G# and not to Ab.

Minor Intervals

A minor interval is **one semitone smaller than a major interval**. Remember, the quality "major" applies only to the 2nd, 3rd, 6th and 7th interval numbers.

This interval is a 6th. In the G major scale, the 6th is E natural. E flat makes the interval smaller by one semitone, so this is a **minor 6th**.

(Don't fall into the trap of thinking that minor intervals occur in minor scales, and major intervals in major scales: this is only half true! While major scales don't contain any minor intervals (built from the tonic), minor scales DO contain major intervals.)

Diminished Intervals

A diminished interval is **one semitone smaller** than a **minor** or **perfect** interval.

A diminished interval is **one tone smaller** than a **major** interval.

- G to C natural is a perfect 4th.
- C flat makes the interval one semitone narrower, so this is a diminished 4th.

- G to F sharp would be a major 7th (think of the G major scale to start with).
- G to F natural is one semitone smaller, so it would be a minor 7th.
- G to F **flat** is two semitones smaller (than a major 7th), so it's a diminished 7th.

Compound Intervals

Intervals which are larger than one octave are called **compound intervals**. There are two ways to describe compound interval numbers:

- by the actual number of notes you count
- by using the word "compound", plus the interval an octave lower.

You can use whichever you prefer.

Compound intervals need to be **qualified** with the word major/minor/perfect/diminished/augmented, in the same way as non-compound intervals. Here is a compound interval:

There are 9 letter names between E and high F, so you can call this a minor 9th. Alternatively, you can call it a "compound minor 2nd", because E to F is a second plus an octave.

What is the interval's quality? (Answer at the bottom of the page!)[2]

TRICKY INTERVALS

This system for working out intervals is easy when you know your major scales. However, some major scales are more awkward than others, and some don't even really exist!

In the first case here, you'd need to know the scale of C# major (awkward, but does exist), and in the second case, you'd need the G## major scale (does not really exist!)

In cases like these, it is usually a good idea to **simplify** the interval. To do this, you need to

- move both notes
- by the same amount
- in the same direction
- without changing the letter name

In the first case, C# major is an awkward scale, but C major is easy. To change C# to C natural, you need to move it **down** by **one semitone.**

You need to move the upper note in the same way, down one semitone. This means A# will become A natural.

Now work out the interval as before: the note A is part of the C major scale, so this is a **major 6th**. The original interval, C#-A# is also a major 6th. (And so is Cb-Ab, of course!)

Let's do the same with the second tricky interval above. The lower note is G##, but G natural would make things a lot simpler.

G## is **two semitones** higher than G natural, so you need to lower G## by a tone to get to G natural. Do the same to the upper note: move D# down by two semitones, without changing the letter name.

You will arrive at Db.

Now compare this interval to the one found in G major. G-D is a perfect 5th, and this is one semitone smaller, so it's a diminished 5th, and therefore, so is G##-D#.

---

[2] Minor

SUMMARY OF INTERVALS:

On the next page is a summary of the technical interval names, in order of size, starting with the smallest, with an example of each, up to a 7th. Octave intervals are the same as unisons, but the upper note is an octave higher. 9ths are the same as 2nds, and so on. One interval is missing. What do you think the interval of C to high Cb is? [3]

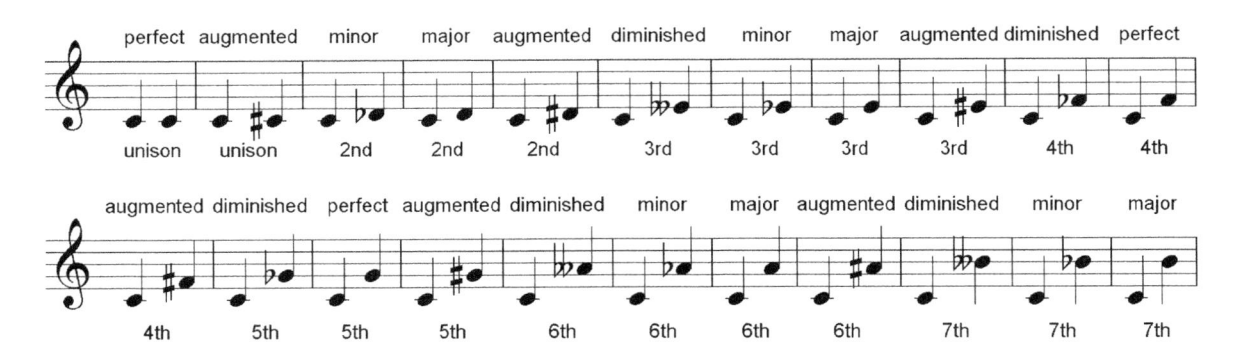

INTERVALS IN A SCORE

In a music theory exam, you might find yourself presented with a real musical score, and get some questions about finding or naming intervals in that score.

There are a few extra things to consider, when you're looking at a real piece of music.

First of all, you need to make sure you know what **clef** is being used. Often, the clef will be the one which you can see right at the beginning of the piece, but it's possible, especially in a piano piece, for the clef to **change** during the piece of music.

In this excerpt for piano, the interval to name is in the box.

Notice that the left hand starts in the bass clef, but then changes to the treble clef in the 2nd bar, so the lower note in this bracketed interval is actually the D just **above** middle C.

When the two interval notes are on different staves, it can be helpful to pencil in the upper note above the lower one, on its stave. This will help you to count up the letter names.

This interval is a minor 7th.

---

[3] Diminished octave

The second thing to watch out for in scores is **accidentals**. You should always check out the **key signature** before starting, of course, but you also need to be on the look-out for accidentals which were written **earlier in the bar**, but still apply.

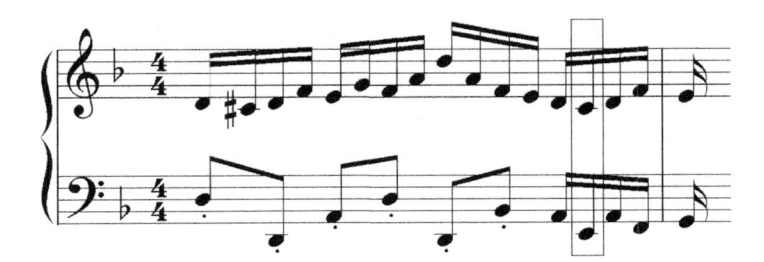

In this excerpt, the boxed interval doesn't contain any accidentals, but if you look earlier in the bar, you'll find there was a C# which will still apply to this note.

This treble clef note is C# just **above** middle C, and the bass clef note is the 2nd E **below** middle C. This is a compound major 6th, or a major 13th.

INTERVALS EXERCISES

Exercise 1 - Perfect Intervals

Look at the following intervals. Decide which are **perfect** and name them as **fourths** or **fifths**. Put a cross next to any intervals which are **not** perfect fourths or perfect fifths.

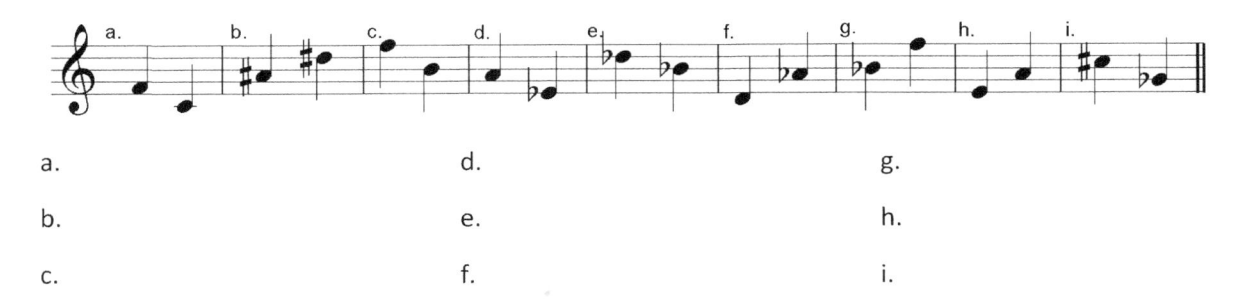

a.

b.

c.

d.

e.

f.

g.

h.

i.

Exercise 2 - Major, Minor and Perfect Intervals

Describe fully each of the numbered melodic intervals (e.g. major 2nd).

a.

b.

c.

d.

e.

f.

g.

h.

i.

j.

k.

l.

m.

n.

o.

p.

q.

r.

s.

t.

Exercise 3 - Augmented and Diminished Intervals

Describe fully each of the numbered melodic intervals (e.g. augmented 2nd).

a.	e.	i.
b.	f.	j.
c.	h.	
d.	h.	

Exercise 4 - Compound Intervals

Describe fully each of the numbered compound melodic intervals (e.g. augmented 9th).

a.	e.	i.
b.	f.	j.
c.	h.	
d.	h.	

Exercise 5 - Mixed Intervals

Describe fully each of the numbered melodic intervals (e.g. augmented 5th).

a.	e.	i.
b.	f.	j.
c.	g.	
d.	h.	

Exercise 6 — Intervals in a Score

Describe fully each of the intervals in the boxes A-D.

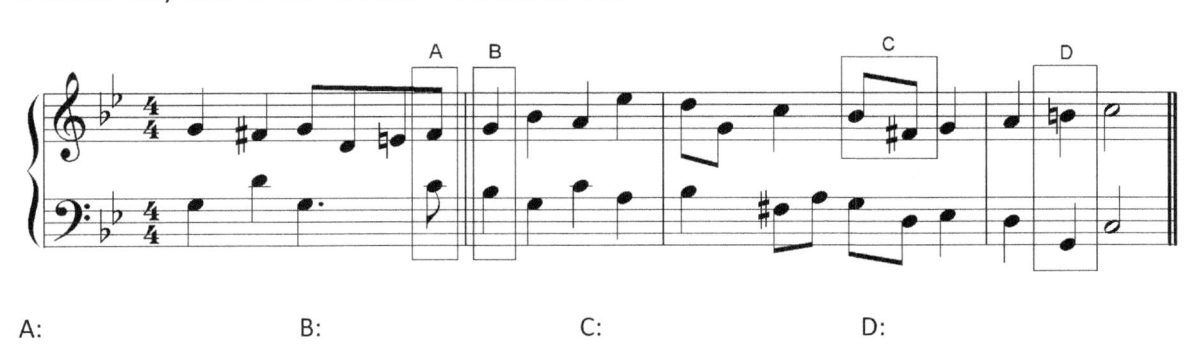

A: B: C: D:

INTERVALS ANSWERS

EXERCISE 1

Perfect 4th   Perfect 4th   X   X   X   X   Perfect 5th   Perfect 4th   X

EXERCISE 2

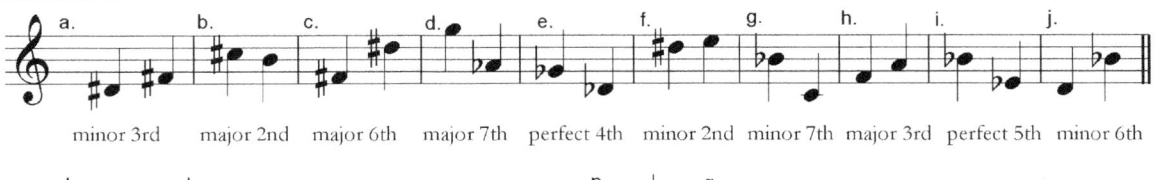

minor 3rd   major 2nd   major 6th   major 7th   perfect 4th   minor 2nd   minor 7th   major 3rd   perfect 5th   minor 6th

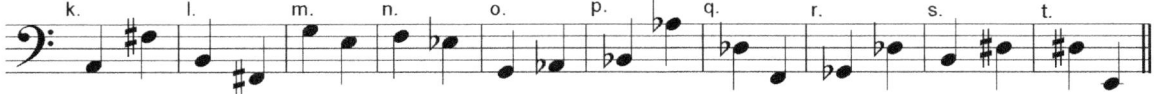

major 6th   perfect 4th   minor 3rd   major 2nd   minor 2nd   minor 7th   minor 6th   perfect 5th   major 3rd   major 7th

EXERCISE 3

dim. 7th   dim. 4th   dim. 5th   aug. 6th   aug. 3rd   dim. 3rd   dim. 6th   aug. 2nd   aug. 4th   aug. 5th

EXERCISE 4

a. maj 9th (compound major 2nd); b. min 13th (compound minor 6th); c. dim 12th (compound dim 5th); d. p. 11th (compound p. 4th); e. min 10th (compound min 3rd); f. aug 9th (compound aug 2nd); g. maj 10th (compound maj 3rd); h. aug 11th (compound aug 4th); i. p. 12th (compound p. 5th); j. min 9th (compound min 2nd)

EXERCISE 5

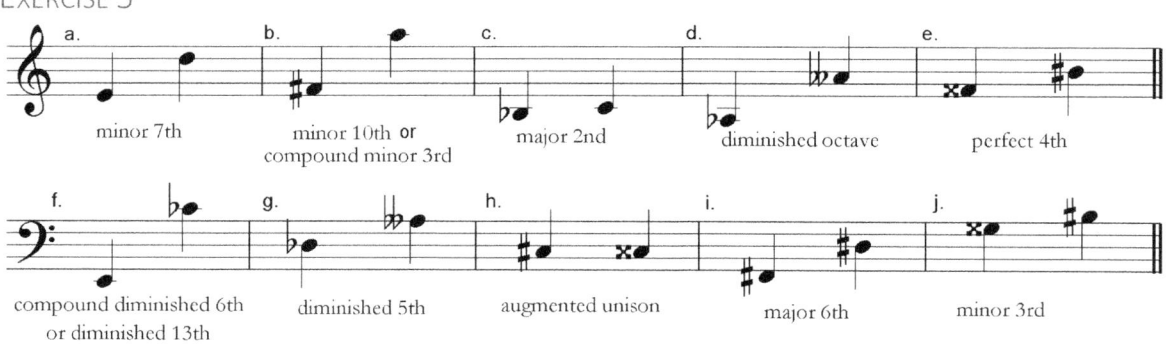

minor 7th   minor 10th or compound minor 3rd   major 2nd   diminished octave   perfect 4th

compound diminished 6th or diminished 13th   diminished 5th   augmented unison   major 6th   minor 3rd

EXERCISE 6

A: Augmented 4th   B: Major 6th   C: Diminished 4th

D: Compound major 3rd (major 10th)

8. TRANSPOSING

TRANSPOSING INSTRUMENTS

What note do you hear when you play this note on the piano?

You hear a middle C, of course. But if you play the same note on a clarinet, horn or trumpet you will hear a **different** note.

Clarinets, horns, trumpets and a few other instruments are "transposing" instruments, which means that the note the player **reads** is different from the note which their instrument **produces**.

For example, if a trumpeter reads and plays the following:

the notes you actually hear are

Most clarinettists start off learning on a "B flat" clarinet. Trumpets are also in B flat. This means that when the player reads a note which looks like a **C**, the note produced by their instrument is actually a **B flat**. Every note that the player reads actually sounds a ton lower.

Some instruments transpose at the octave, which means that this note

would sound as a C, but not **middle** C. It could be an octave higher (for the piccolo, for example), or lower (e.g. for the double bass).

WHY ARE THERE TRANSPOSING INSTRUMENTS?

There are many different reasons why we have transposing instruments, and most of them are very interesting. However, you don't need to know **why** for Grade 5 Theory! If you're interested and would like to find out, read about them here: http://en.wikipedia.org/wiki/Transposing_instrument

COMMON TRANSPOSING INSTRUMENTS

These are the transposing instruments you need to know about for grade 5 theory:

- Clarinet - in B flat and A
- Trumpet - in B flat
- Horn and cor Anglais - in F

In each case, the key of the instrument is the note which is produced when the player reads a **C**.

GRADE 5 THEORY QUESTION TYPES

As well as having to transpose extracts of music (see below), you might also need to know a bit of general knowledge about all the common orchestral instruments and which octaves they play in. Often you are asked to choose one instrument (from four) which could play a given extract, so that it sounds at the **same pitch**.

So, you need to learn which instruments can play each other's music because the **clef** is the same and there is no change in **pitch**. Try to memorise the following groups of instruments, which might appear in the grade 5 theory exam:

Transposition/Clef	Instruments
Non-transposing, treble clef	Flute, Oboe, Violin
Non-transposing, bass clef.	Bassoon, Cello, Trombone, Tuba
Octave-down transposing, bass clef	Double Bass
In B flat, treble clef	Bb Clarinet, Trumpet
In F, treble clef	Horn, Cor Anglais
Non-transposing, in alto clef	Viola

Sometimes you will see drum-type instruments included in the choices, "timpani", for example. Kettle drums (timpani) are only tuned to one note, which means they can't play a melody - they will never be the right answer to the question!

What is "concert pitch"?

The term "concert pitch" means the **real** sound of a note, as you would get on the piano. (On the piano if you read/play a C, you hear a C, if you read/play an F sharp you hear an F sharp, and so on).

Players of transposing instruments look at notes in two ways - the name they give to a note is not the same as the way it sounds. A trumpet player reads/fingers/plays a C, but the note he plays is a **concert pitch** B flat, because that note corresponds to a B flat on the piano (or any other non-transposing instrument).

When an orchestra tunes up, all the players play **concert pitch** A. This means that clarinettists and trumpet players finger a B, and horn players finger an E.

Transposing a Melody for a Transposing Instrument

You might have to transpose a melody into (or out of) concert pitch. In Grade 5 Theory, you will always be told which **direction** you have to transpose in (up or down), and by what **interval** (major 2nd, perfect 5th etc.) (You don't have to work out from scratch how to write out a piece of clarinet music so that it sounds at concert pitch, for example!)

You will need to understand **intervals** properly before you can begin. (Have a look at "Lesson 7 – Intervals" if you need to). Sometimes you are asked to use a key signature, and sometimes not. Read the question carefully!

Transposing with a Key Signature

If you have been asked to include a key signature, start by carefully transposing it and writing the new key signature on the stave.

For example, if the key signature is **A major** (3 sharps) and you have been asked to transpose **down a major 2nd**, you will need to write the key signature for **G major** (1 sharp), because G is a major 2nd lower than A.

(You don't need to work out whether the piece is in a major or minor key - just assume it is in a major one, then transpose the key signature. If the piece below, with 3 sharps in the key signature, was actually in F# minor, then to transpose the key signature you would bring it down by a major 2nd to E minor. E minor also has one sharp, the same as G major - so it makes no difference!)

Don't forget to add the time signature (this doesn't change, of course).

Let's transpose this melody down a major 2nd, using a key signature.

It starts off like this:

Next, transpose each note in turn. Be careful when you come across accidentals - in the above extract the first accidental is **E sharp**. Transpose E sharp down a major second, and you get **D sharp**.

(If you think that E sharp on a piano keyboard is the same as F, you might think the correct transposition would be E flat - but you would be wrong: E sharp - E flat is actually an interval of a double-augmented unison!)

Here is the finished transposition:

When you transpose with a key signature, the accidentals always fall in the **same** place as in the original melody. There were three accidentals in the above melody, and there are three in the transposition. (In this case, the natural is a "courtesy" accidental and is there as a reminder). They might, however, be different accidentals, for example a sharp might change into a natural.

For example, if you had a C# written as an accidental in G major, and you transposed everything down a major 2nd, the new key would be F major, and the C# would become B **natural**. Sketch out a piano keyboard to help you, if necessary.

Transposing Without a Key Signature

If you are asked to transpose **without** using a key signature, you will need to be very careful. Check each note as you write it, making sure that the intervals are exactly correct.

Here is a melody which needs to be transposed upwards by a minor 3rd, **without using a key signature.**

First, write in all the notes, one third higher. Concentrate on putting the notes in the correct spaces/lines. We will add the accidentals in a moment. You might need to change the stem direction of some notes.

Which note stems had to change direction?

Next, check **each note in turn**. Keep an eye on the key signature and any accidentals in the original. Sketch out a mini-piano keyboard, if it helps!

The first note is F. Put that up a minor third, and you get Ab, so put a flat on the left-hand side of the first A.

Use the keyboard sketch to make sure that you have the same number of semitones between each original and transposed note (3 semitones, in this case).

Continue in the same way, adding all necessary accidentals. Don't forget: when an accidental is placed in bar, it also affects all other notes of the same pitch in that bar.

Here is the rest of the transposition.

Avoiding Mistakes

Lightly pencil (in the margin of your exam paper) a list of the letter names from the extract and what they will **become**. When you've finished, carefully double check each note. (You can also make sure you've transposed to the right key signature using this list). Your list could look something like this:

	D	E	E #	F #	G #	A	B	B #	C #
becomes	C	D	D #	E	F #	G	A	A #	B

If you are told that the melody was written, for example, for "clarinet in Bb", don't fall into the trap of thinking the **key** of music is Bb - you need to check the **key signature** to work out the key.

"Clarinet in Bb" simply means that the instrument plays **concert pitch** Bb when the note C is read.

97

Spotting Transposition Mistakes

In the new (2020 onwards) online ABRSM exams, you will probably be asked to look at a bar of transposed music, and to say whether parts of it are correct or not.

Look carefully at the key signature. Think of the major key that uses this time signature (e.g. "F major"), then transpose that keynote (F) in the way the question asks. For example, if the transposition is "down a minor 3rd", then transpose F down a minor 3rd, to D. The new key signature should be that for D major. If it says "up a minor 3rd", the new key signature should be Ab major.

Look at each note in turn, and transpose each note in the same way, so that you know what the correct transposition should be, then look at the given bar to check whether it is correct or not. Don't forget to think about notes that are affected by the key signature, and accidentals.

Here is an example. Here is a bar written for clarinet in A.

This is a transposition into concert pitch, down a minor 3rd. There are some mistakes – put a tick or cross to show what is correct/incorrect.

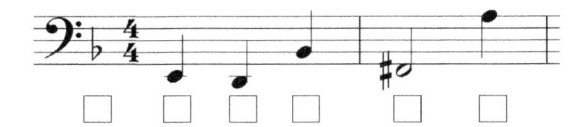

Key signature: the original was Bb major. A minor 3rd down from Bb is G, so the new key signature should have one sharp, not one flat. (You could think of the original as G minor, which would be E minor when transposed down a minor 3rd. E minor also has a key signature of one sharp).

Note 1: G down a minor 3rd is E, so this note is correct.

Note 2: F# down a minor 3rd is D#, so this note is incorrect.

Note 3: D down a minor 3rd is B, so this note is incorrect (because the key signature makes it Bb).

Note 4: A down a minor 3rd is F#, so this note is correct.

Note 5: Bb down a minor 3rd is G, so this note is incorrect.

TRANSPOSING EXERCISES
Exercise 1 - Transposing with a Key Signature

a. The following melody is written for clarinet in B flat. Transpose it **down** a major 2nd, as it will sound at concert pitch. Use a key signature and remember to put in all necessary sharp, flat or natural signs.

b. The following melody is written for horn in F. Transpose it **down** a perfect 5th, as it will sound at concert pitch. Use a key signature and remember to put in all necessary sharp, flat or natural signs.

EXERCISE 2 - TRANSPOSING WITHOUT A KEY SIGNATURE

a. These are the actual sounds made by a clarinet in A. Transpose it **up** a minor 3rd. Do **not** use a key signature but remember to put in all the necessary sharp, flat or natural signs.

b. These are the actual sounds made by a horn in F. Transpose it **up** a perfect 5th. Do **not** use a key signature but remember to put in all the necessary sharp, flat or natural signs.

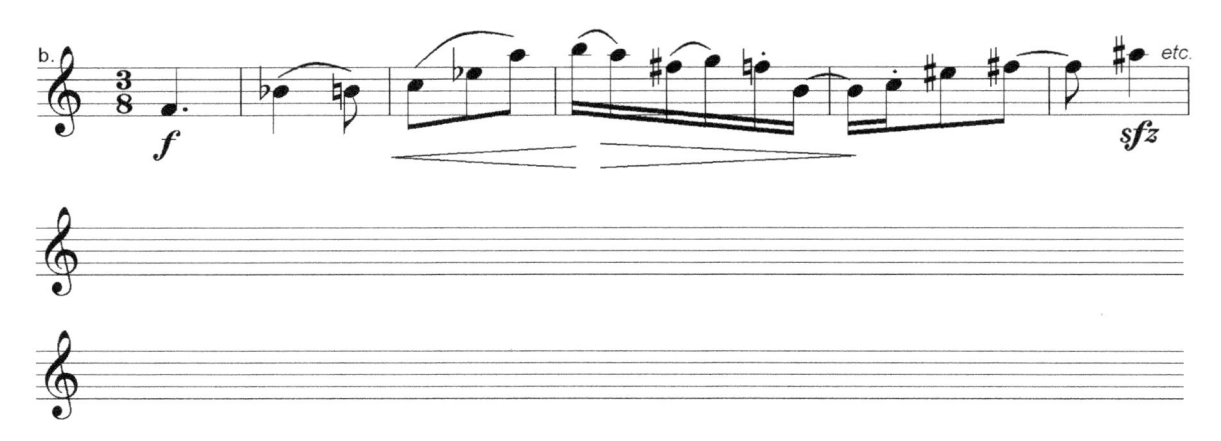

EXERCISE 3 – SPOTTING ERRORS

Put a tick or cross to show whether these transpositions are correct:

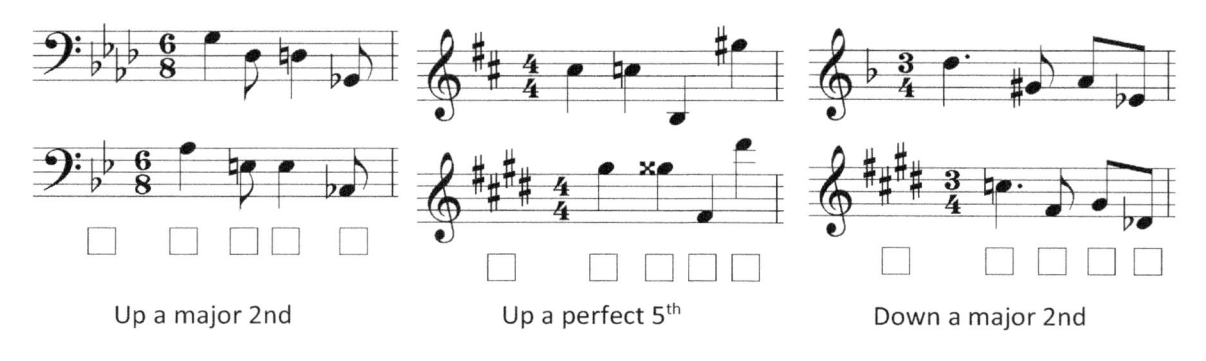

Up a major 2nd   Up a perfect 5th   Down a major 2nd

100

TRANSPOSITION ANSWERS

EXERCISE 1

EXERCISE 2

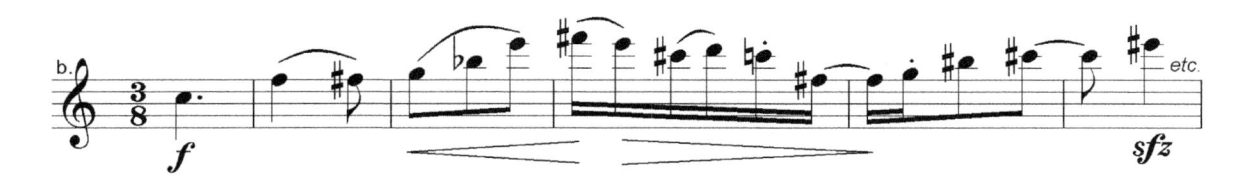

EXERCISE 3

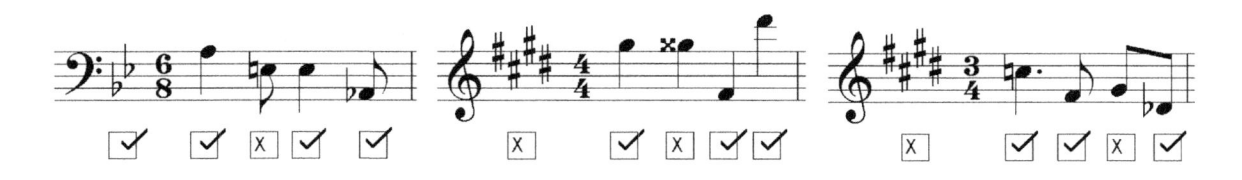

9. CHORDS

Chords

A chord is a group of notes which sound at the same time. Chords are usually made up of three basic notes, (but any of the notes can be **doubled up** without changing the type of chord).

To make chords, we first need to decide which **key** we are in. Let's take the key of C major as an example. Here's the C major scale.

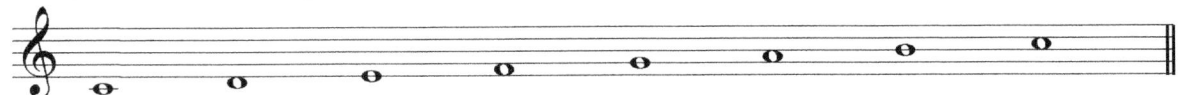

To make a chord, we choose one of the notes of the scale and add **another two** notes above it. The note we start on is called the **root**. The notes we add are the **third** and the **fifth**. (See "Lesson 7: Intervals" for more about intervals). This gives us seven different chords. Here are those chords in C major.

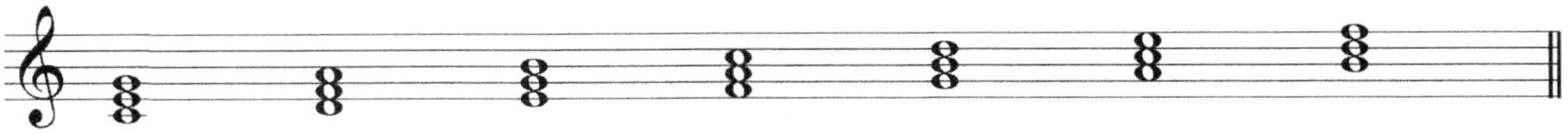

Triads

These basic chords are also known as **triads**. A triad is always made up of a root, a third above the root, and a fifth above the root. Notice that the notes of these triads are either **all** on lines, or **all** in spaces. Triads/chords can be **major, minor, diminished** or **augmented**.

Here are the chords in C major with their names:

C major · D minor · E minor · F major · G major · A minor · B diminished

In a minor key, the chords are built from the notes of the **harmonic minor scale**. This means you always have to raise the 7th degree of the scale by a semitone.

Here are the chords in A minor with their names:

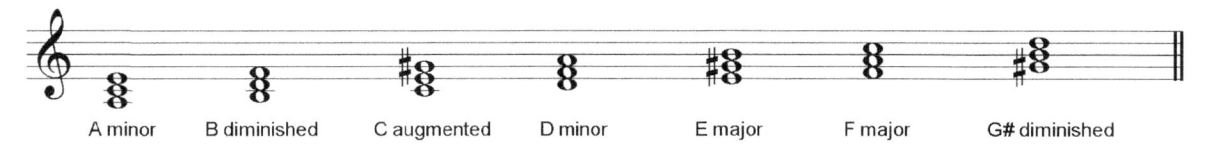

A minor · B diminished · C augmented · D minor · E major · F major · G# diminished

Major chords are made with a **major** third and a perfect fifth above the root.

Minor chords are made with a **minor** third and a perfect fifth above the root.

Diminished chords contain a minor third and a **diminished** fifth above the root.

Augmented chords contain a major third and an **augmented** fifth. You don't need to use any augmented chords in the Grade 5 Theory exam though!

Naming Chords

We also use **Roman numerals** or **technical names** to name chords.

The Roman numerals 1-7 are I, II, III, IV, V VI and VII.

(Major chords are sometimes written with capital Roman numerals, whereas minor chords are written with small letters. You can write them all with capitals in your grade 5 theory exam.)

Here are the C major chords with their Roman numeral names:

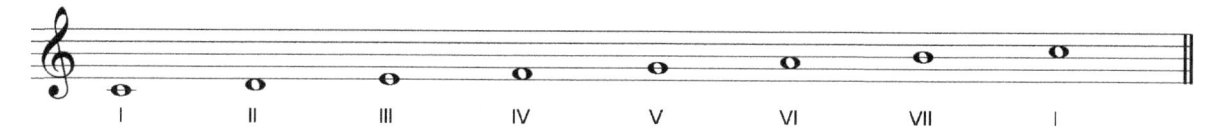

We also use the technical names **tonic, supertonic, mediant, subdominant, dominant, submediant and leading note**, to refer to the same chords. Chord V is the **dominant chord**, for example.

Do you have to learn all these chords for Grade 5 Theory?

No! In Grade 5 Theory, you only have to know chords **I, II, IV and V**.

In a major key, **I, IV and V** are major chords but **II** is a minor chord.

In a minor key, **I and IV** are minor, **II** is diminished, and **V** is major and includes an accidental (because of the raised 7th of the scale).

Inversions

In all the chords we've looked at so far, the lowest note in the chord was the **root**.

When the root is the lowest note, the chord is in **root position**.

Chords can also be **inverted** (turned upside down).

When a chord is "inverted" the position of the notes is changed around so that the **lowest** note of the chord is the **third** or the **fifth**, rather than the root.

Here are some inversions chord I in **C** major (which contains the notes C, E and G).

Lowest note is E (the third)   Lowest note is G (the fifth)

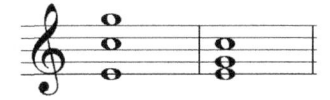

It **doesn't** matter what order the **higher** notes are in: inversions are defined by the **lowest note** of the chord. This note is also known as the **bass note**. Make sure you understand the difference between the terms "bass note" and "root". The root is the lowest note of the triad when it is written in its basic form. The bass note is the lowest note you can **hear** when the chord is played.

Naming Inversions

In the UK, we use the letters **a**, **b** and **c** (written in lower case letters) to describe the **lowest** note of a chord.

When the chord is in **root position** (hasn't been inverted), we use the letter **a**.

When the lowest note is the third, (e.g. E in C major), we use the letter **b**. This is also called **first inversion**.

When the lowest note is the fifth, (e.g. G in C major), we use the letter **c**. This is also called **second inversion**.

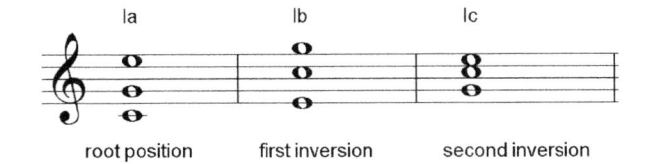

Here is chord I in C major, in three different positions:

Figured Bass

Chords are sometimes written in **figured bass**, which is a system that uses numbers to describe notes of a chord.

Each figure has two numbers in it. The numbers refer to the intervals above the **bass note** (lowest note) of the chord. Examples are given for a C major chord.

is used for root position (a) chords. Above the bass note (C), there is a note a 3rd higher (E), and another which is a 5th higher (G).

is used for first inversion (b) chords. Above the bass note (E), there is a note a 3rd higher (G), and another which is a 6th higher (C).

is used for second inversion (c) chords. Above the bass note (G), there is a note a 4th higher (C) and another which is a 6th higher (E).

How to Identify Chords in a Piece of Music

In the Grade 5 Theory exam, you might be asked to identify some chords within a piece of music. The question will tell you what **key** the music is in.

You need to

1. Pick out which notes make up the chord
2. Work out what the name of the chord is
3. Work out what inversion the chord is in

That's a lot to do all in one go, so we'll break it down into steps!

1. Picking out the Notes of the Chord

Chords are often not as easy to spot as in our examples above. They can include a mix of notes of different lengths, a mix of instruments, different staves and even a combination of clefs.

Look at **all** the notes in the chord which are enclosed in the **bracket**.

There might be several notes, but there will only be **3 different note names**. If you have an extract for more than one instrument, don't forget to look in **all** the parts. You might also get a tied note from a previous bar with an accidental that is still relevant - look very carefully.

The following bar, (for cello and piano), is in F major: the chords you need to describe are in brackets, marked **A** and **B**:

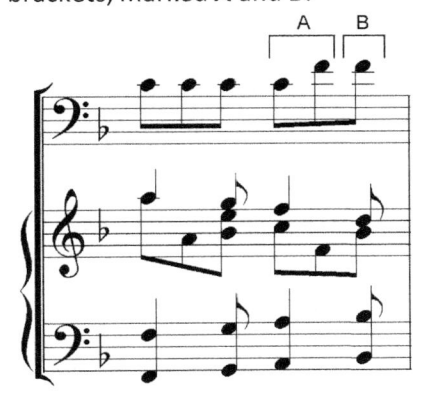

Notice that chord A is split over **two** quaver (eighth note) beats, and both chords are split across all **three** staves.

- Chord **A** has the notes A, C, and F
- Chord **B** has the notes B flat, D and F.

Now you have picked out the notes of the chords, you are ready to **name** them.

Naming Chords

We work out the chord name by finding the **root position** (a) chord.

The root position of the chord is where the three notes are **as close together as possible**. The three notes will be an interval of **a third** from each other.

- In chord A (above), we have the notes A, C and F. The closest way of putting these together is F-A-C. (There is a third between F and A, and another third between A and C).

  The first note from F-A-C is F, so this is a chord of F. The interval F-A is a **major** third, so it's an F major chord. Remember that the extract is in F (major), so this is chord I.

- In chord B (above), we have the notes Bb-D-F. This is the closest they can be: Bb to D is a third, and D to F is a third.

  The first note from Bb-D-F is Bb, so this is a chord of Bb. Bb-D is a major third, so it's a Bb major chord.

  Bb is the 4th note in the key of F major, so this is chord IV.

Working out Inversions

Finally, we need to work out the **inversion.** You need to look at the **lowest sounding** note of the chord.

- If the lowest note is the **same** as the chord name itself, it will be **"a"**, (root position).
- If the lowest note is the **third** it will be **"b"**, (first inversion).
- And if it's the **fifth** it will be **"c"**, (second inversion).

Let's look at our above examples.

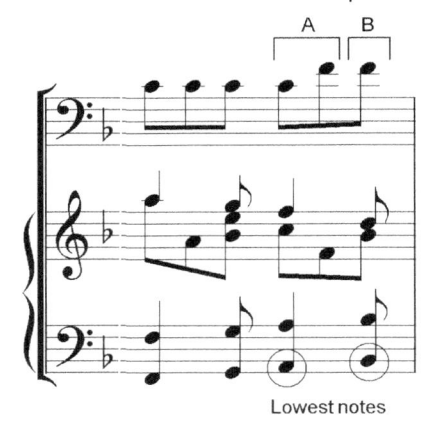

Chord **A**'s lowest note is A. The chord is F major, so the lowest note is the third. So, this chord is **b**. Its full name is **Ib**. It's a first inversion chord.

Chord **B**'s lowest note is B flat and it is a chord of B flat, so it's in root position. This chord is **a**. Its full name is **IVa**.

Common Mistakes

Don't forget to check what key the extract is in - the instructions will tell you this information.

Check back to see if the **key signature** or any **accidentals** affect the notes you are looking at.

Make sure you include all the notes which are sounding on the beat which is marked. Sometimes the chord will include a note that started earlier in a bar but is **still** sounding. Here are two examples:

This chord (marked with a bracket) is the third beat of the bar.

However, the lowest note is the left-hand B flat, which is played on the first beat but is **still sounding** (circled).

This chord is the second beat of the bar.

Apart from the right-hand G and left-hand B flat, the chord also includes the right-hand E flat crotchet (quarter note), which is **still sounding** from the first beat of the bar.

Did you notice the left hand is playing in the treble clef?

USING CHORDS TO WORK OUT KEY

The key of a piece of music is fixed by the **harmony**, or the chords which make up the accompaniment.

Even when there is only a single, solo melody, the melody notes will combine to fit with certain chords. Although we might not hear the chords being played, our brains understand which chords are **implied** (suggested) by the melody.

The **tonic** and **dominant** chords are the two chords which work together to fix a key. If a melody does not closely fit the tonic and dominant chords at the beginning of a piece, our brains have a hard time understanding what the key is supposed to be, and the music sounds vague.

(Some more modern composers do this on purpose, but for the moment we will learn about the rules before breaking them!)

So, in order to be 100% certain of the key of a piece of music, you need to look at the harmony (or implied harmony). When a piece of music begins, chords I and V are normally used right at the beginning, to firmly fix the key.

If a piece of music changes key (also called "modulating") these two chords are also used to fix the new key.

In the lesson on key signatures, we learned that the key of a piece of music can sometimes be worked out by seeing which scale the notes of the melody belong to.

We also learned that this method doesn't always work – but why not?

Each key signature belongs to two keys – a major and a minor one. This means that most of the notes in C major (for example) also exist in A minor. What makes A minor different from C major?

In the melodic minor scale, we raise the 6th and 7th degrees of the **ascending** scale (F# and G# in A minor melodic). This means we sometimes see F# and G# in A minor pieces, which does help to differentiate them from C major.

However, in the A minor melodic **descending** scale, we find F natural and G natural, which means it uses **exactly the same** notes as the C major scale – the difference is only the start and end note, which we call the **tonic**.

The tonic note is **very important** then, and so is the **tonic chord**. The **dominant** note/chord is the second most important.

We expect to find these notes, or the scales or chords they make, in the most important positions in the music. These include:

- The first note
- The first complete bar
- Notes which fall on the main beats of the bar in bar 1

In the following piece of music (which is from a Minuet by Haydn), you might think it's in A minor at first glance, since it seems to use the notes of the A minor harmonic scale.

However, the first note G is not in the tonic or dominant chord in A minor.

Don't forget, the dominant chord is always major because we base it on the harmonic minor scale, so in A minor the dominant chord is E-G#-B.

The notes in bar 1 combine into a chord of C major.

These are two strong clues that the piece is actually in C major, not A minor.

Play it and see! The G# in bar 2 is there for "decoration", or, because it sounds nice!

CHORDS EXERCISES

Exercise 1: Naming Chords on One Stave

Describe the following chords as I, II, IV or V. Also indicate whether the lowest note of the chord is the root (a), 3rd (b) or 5th (c). The key is given.

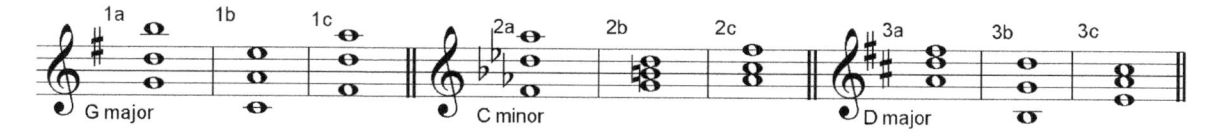

Exercise 2: Naming Chords on Two Staves

Describe the following chords marked in brackets as I, II, IV or V. Also indicate whether the lowest note of the chord is the root (a), 3rd (b) or 5th (c).

a) This is a Bagatelle by Beethoven, Op.119 No.11. The key is Bb major.

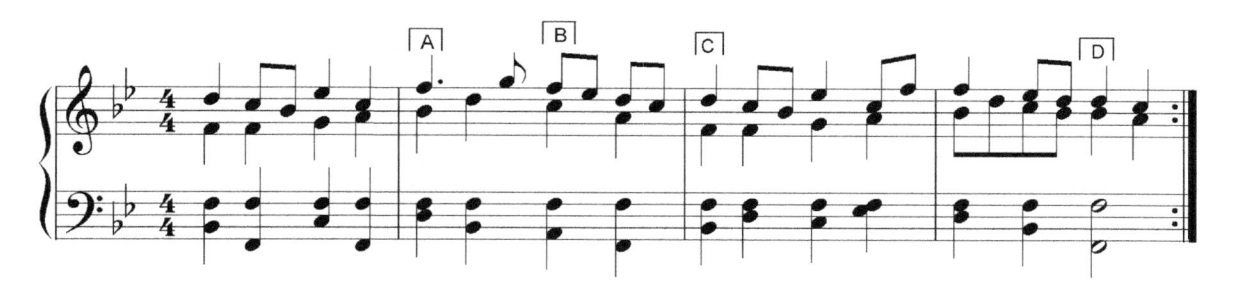

b) This is adapted from Chorale no.47 by JS Bach. The key is D minor.

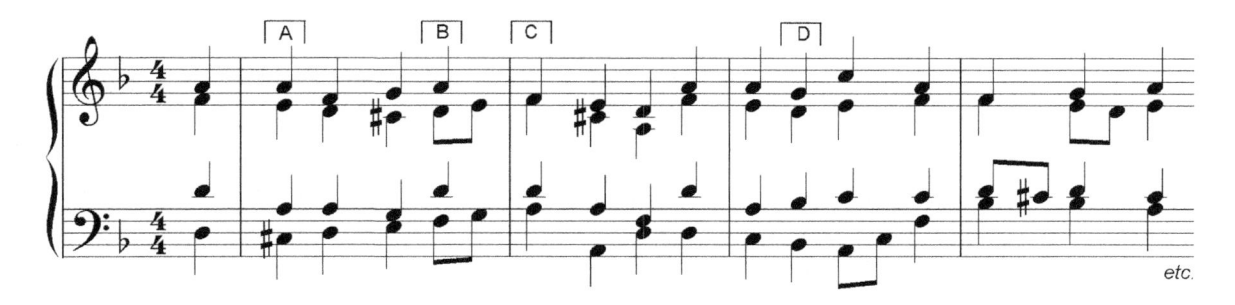

EXERCISE 3: NAMING CHORDS OVER THREE STAVES

Describe the following chords marked in brackets as I, II, IV or V. Also indicate whether the lowest note of the chord is the root (a), 3rd (b) or 5th (c).

a) This is adapted from Handel's Violin Sonata, Op.1 No.10, 3rd Movement. The key is G minor.

b) This is adapted from Crusell's Clarinet Concerto, Op.11, Andante Moderato. The key is Eb major.

EXERCISE 4

Identify the key of each of these tunes, by working out the implied harmony.

110

CHORDS ANSWERS

Exercise 1

1a: Ia   2a: IIb   3a: Ic
1b: IIb   2b: Va   3b: IVb
1c: Vb   2c: IVb   3c: Vc

Exercise 2

a)   b)

A: Ib   A: Vb

B: Vb   B: Ib

C: Ia   C: Ic

D: Ic   D: IVb

Exercise 3a

A: IVb

B: Va

C: Ib

Exercise 3b

A: Ia

B: Vb

C: IIb

D: Ic

Exercise 4

a. D minor

b. F minor

c. A major

10. PROGRESSIONS AND CADENCES

(Please note: you need to know about chords (see lesson 10) to understand this lesson.)

WHAT ARE PROGRESSIONS?

In music, a "progression" happens when one chord changes to another chord.

For example, many pieces of music begin with notes that are taken from **chord I** (the tonic chord), followed by notes from **chord V** (the dominant chord).

Here is the beginning of the famous theme from Dvorak's "New World Symphony", which begins with a I-V progression.

The key of the piece is D major (we have simplified the key, as the original is in Db major!)

The notes in bar 1 fit with a chord of D major, which is chord I, and the notes in bar two fit with a chord of A major, which is chord V.

Notice that the melody also contains notes which are **not** part of the underlying harmony chord. In bar 1, there is an E, which isn't part of the chord of D major. And in bar 2, there are two F#s, which are not part of the chord of A major. These are **non-chord** notes.

The notes which fall **on the stronger beat** are always[4] chord notes. (Notes which fall on an **off-beat** can be either chord notes or non-chord notes: more about this later.)

In the above example, the time signature is 4/4. This means there are four crotchet (quarter note) beats per bar. The notes which are played at the start of each of those four main beats are all chord notes:

In bar one, the notes which fall on the beat are F#-A-F#-D. These are all notes in the chord of D major.

In bar two, the notes which fall on the beat are E-A-E. These are both notes in A major. (The C# is missing, but that is ok!)

You only need to know about progressions which use the chords **I, II, IV** and **V** for Grade 5 Theory.

---

[4] "always" refers to "in the grade 5 music theory exam". In real life, non-chord notes sometimes also fall on the beat, but this is covered in grade 6 and above.

Some progressions are very common, and others are very rarely used. You should always use the common progressions, not the rare ones, in your theory exam.

- Chord I can move to any chord
- Chord V normally only moves to chord I (chord VI is also possible, but we don't use chord VI at this grade).
- Chord V does not normally move to chord IV or II.
- Chord IV can move to any chord.
- Chord II can move to chord V or IV but not chord I

What are Cadences?

Cadences are special kinds of progression which are used to signify that a piece, or section/phrase of a piece, has come to an **end**.

There are only three cadences that you need to know for Grade 5 Theory. Here they are:

V - I (also known as a "perfect" cadence)

IV - I (also known as a "plagal" cadence)

? - V (also known as an "imperfect" cadence)

As you can see, all cadences finish with either chord I or chord V. This is very important to remember!

In an "imperfect" cadence we have used a question mark for the first chord, because, in fact, any chord can be used before V. Most commonly, you will find I, II, IV or VI. You don't need chord VI in Grade 5 theory, so the there are three different imperfect cadences at this grade: I-V, II-V and IV-V.

Here is an example in C major. The first phrase ends with cadence 1, and the piece ends with cadence 2.

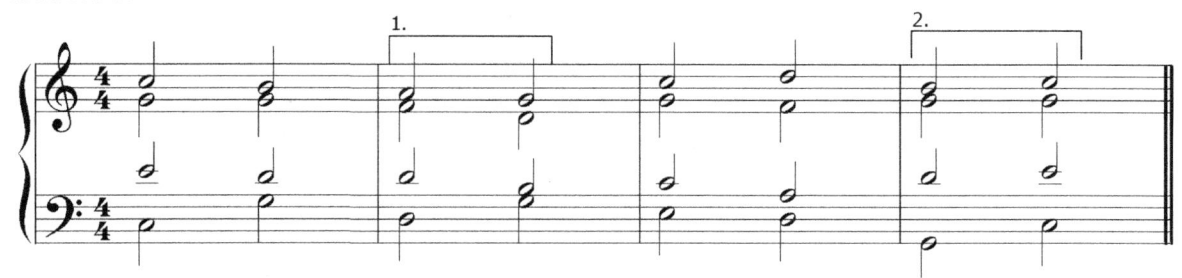

Cadence 1 progresses from a chord of D minor to G major- or **II-V** (imperfect).

Cadence 2 progresses from a chord of G major to C major- or **V-I** (perfect).

Here are the same cadences from above, but fitted to a melody line and with some added decoration in the other parts:

In the ABRSM grade 5 exam, you may be asked to identify a cadence by name (perfect, imperfect or plagal). The questions use major keys only.

Here is an example- what is the name of the cadence shown in the bracket?

First identify the key (look at the key signature): *this is A major*

Write down the notes in triads I, II, IV and V: *chord I=A-C#-E, chord II=B-D-F#, chord IV=D-F#-A and chord V=E-G#-B.*

Now look at the notes in each chord, to see which chord it is. *The first chord is made up of the notes E, G# and B, so this is chord V. The second chord uses A, C# and E, so this is chord I.*

Now look at the two chords together: *V-I is the pattern for a perfect cadence.*

(Tip: usually the chords in are root position, so you can actually just look at the bass notes (lowest notes: E-A) and then compare them to the degrees of the scale. E is the 5th note in A major, and A is the 1st note, so the chords are V-I.)

114

Progression Questions

In Grade 5 Theory, you are given a melody line and are asked to suggest suitable chords for two or three **progressions**.

Each progression will consist of **two or three chords** and must include a standard **cadence**.

Remember, all cadences are made up of **two chords**. So, if there are three chords in the question, the first one will not be part of the cadence, but part of the progression.

The positions of the cadences are marked in the score; you have to work out which chords would best fit around the notes in the melody at the points indicated.

Let's take the melody we used above as an example. This is what the question might look like:

Suggest suitable progressions for two cadences in the following melody by indicating ONLY ONE chord (I, II, IV or V) at each of the places marked A-E. You do not have to indicate the position of the chords, or to state which note is in the bass.

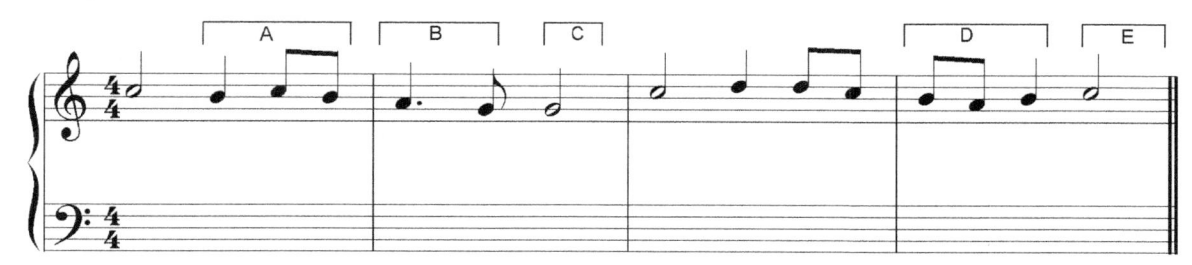

First Cadence: A= ...... B= ...... C= ....   Second Cadence: D= ...... E= ......

In this case, the first **progression** has three chords: A, B and C. The **cadence** is actually chords B and C. The second progression has only two chords, so both of them also make up the cadence.

You can indicate your choice of chords either by either by

- using the Roman numeral system (e.g. **IV**) (recommended), or
- writing the notes of the chord directly onto the stave (more chance of making a mistake!)

You **don't** need to indicate the inversion of the chord (i.e. you don't need to say what position it is in, or which note is in the bass).

Method for Suggesting Suitable Chords

To work out the correct chords, follow these steps. More guidance is given for each step below.

1. Identify the key signature
2. Write down the notes of each of the chords I, II, IV and V in that key signature.
3. Identify which notes are enclosed by the bracket.
4. Decide which are chord notes, and which are non-chord notes.
5. Identify the possible chords and select the most likely if there seems to be a choice.

1. Identify the Key Signature

Using the key signature, work out which two keys (major and minor) it might be. E.g. if there is one sharp, it might be G major or E minor.

- If there **aren't** any sharps or naturals added, it will **probably** be in a major key.
- If there are sharps or naturals, one will usually be on the **leading note**. The semitone **after** the leading note is the tonic of the corresponding minor key. E.g. in A minor, we'd expect to find a G#.
- Sing through the melody in your head and think about whether it sounds major or minor
- Look at the first and last notes – they'll normally be the tonic or dominant notes of the key the piece is in. E.g. in the example above, the piece starts and ends on the tonic of C major.

(Check Lesson 5 - Key Signatures if you need more help on this.)

2. Write Down the Chords

Write down the notes which make up the chords **I**, **II**, **IV** and **V** in the key signature of the piece (this is a good way to avoid mistakes!) You will use this for reference.

For example, if the key is D major, write:

I= D/F#/A   IV= G/B/D

II= E/G/B   V= A/C#/E

3. Identify the Bracketed Notes

Look at the first place marked in the extract. You will see a bracket which encloses 1-5 **different** notes. Write these notes down in letters, and then double check to see if there any accidentals which need to be applied. Check the key signature, tied notes and accidentals which occur earlier in the bar.

4. Identify the Chord Notes

As we mentioned at the start of this lesson, notes which fall **on the stronger beat** are chord notes. This means that the first note in the bracketed group **must** be part of the chord, because the bracket will always start on a note which is on a stronger beat. So, the first note is always a **chord note**.

If the next note is an interval of a **2nd** away from the first note (i.e. a scale-step), it will be a **non-chord** note. If it is any other interval away, then it will be a **chord note**.

In these examples, the first note D is a chord note. The 2nd (boxed) note is sometimes a chord note, and sometimes a non-chord note.

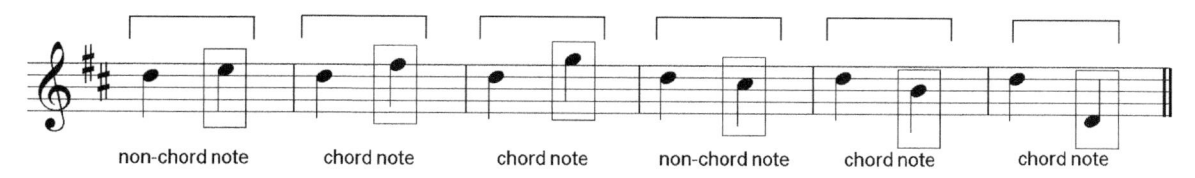

If there is a third note (or fourth, fifth and so on!), apply the same logic: if it is a 2nd away from the last chord note, it will be a non-chord note. If it's not a 2nd away, it will be a chord note.

The notes marked with a star here are all chord notes.

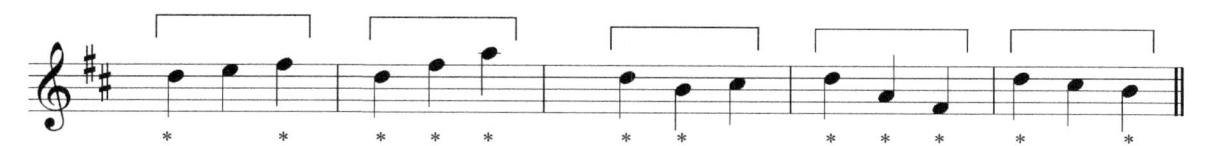

In bar 1, the E is a non-chord note because it is a **2nd** away from D. The F# is a 3rd from D, so it is also a chord note.

In bar 2, the F# is a third from D, so it's a chord note. The A is a third from F# (the last chord note), so it's also a chord note.

In bar 3, the B is a third from D, so it's a chord note. The C# is a **2nd** from B (the last chord note), so it's a non-chord note.

See if you can work out the logic for bars 4 and 5 yourself.

5. Select the Chords

All the notes which you identified as **chord notes** in step 4 **must** be part of the chord you select.

Remember that all cadences end with only **chord I or chord V**: this narrows down the choice for the last chord in each progression.

If the last chord is I, then the one before it can only be V (perfect cadence) or IV (plagal cadence). V-I is much more common than IV-I.

Progressions have to **progress!** This means you cannot immediately repeat the same chord (e.g. V-V) even if the notes seem to fit.

Working Through a Question

Now let's use the method to find the chords from our original example.

The first progression is made up of chords A, B and C, and the second is chords D and E.

The key is C major, because there is no key signature and there are no accidentals, and it starts and ends on the tonic.

We'll write out the notes of the chords for easy reference:

I=C/E/G   II=D/F/A   IV=F/A/C   V=G/B/D

Next, we'll work out which are the chord notes. Chord notes are shown in square brackets at the end of each sentence below.

Chord A: The first note is B, so this must be in the chord. C is a non-chord note (it's a 2nd from B). [B]

Chord B: The first note is A, so this is a chord note. G is a 2nd from A, so it's a non-chord note. [A]

Chord C: G is the only note! [G]

Chord D: B is the first note. A is a 2nd away. [B]

Chord E: C is the only note! [C]

Finally, select the chords. Remember, we are restricted to I and V for the last chord in each progression, so start at the ends!

Chord C: The note G fits with both I and V. Chord B: The note A fits with II and IV.

This means that there are two possible cadences: chords B and C could be II-V (imperfect) or IV-I (plagal).

Chord A: The note B fits with only chord V.

So, for the first progression, A=V, B=II and C=V or as an alternative, A=V, B=IV and C=I.

(Remember, chord V does not normally move to chord IV, so V-IV-V is not a good answer).

In the second progression, again we start at the end:

Chord E: The note C fits with chord I, but not chord V.

(If chord E is I, then chord D can only be V (perfect cadence) or IV (plagal cadence).)

Chord D: The note B fits with V. So, for the second progression, D=V and E=I.

Here's another question, this time a little more complicated:

See if you can work it out for yourself, then read the next paragraph to see if you (and your logic) were right!

Answer

A: Chord II (C minor). The chord notes are G-C-Eb.

B: Chord V (F major). This is the first chord of a V-I (perfect) cadence. The chord notes are F and A.

C: Chord I (Bb major). This is the second chord of a V-I (perfect) cadence. Only chords I and V can be used in this place, and Bb is only in chord I, not chord V.

D: Chord IV (Eb major). Although Eb is in chord II as well, there is no cadence which ends II-I.

E: Chord I (Bb major). D is only in chord I, and cadences can only end with I or V.

Check out the mymusictheory.com video on cadences at
https://www.youtube.com/watch?v=vtAwpynolz8

PROGRESSIONS AND CADENCES EXERCISES

Exercise 1: Questions about Progressions and Cadences

1. How many chords make up a cadence?

2. What is the difference between a progression and a cadence?

3. Using Roman numerals, give the five acceptable cadences you can use in the Grade 5 exam.

4. When is a melody note considered to be a **non-chord** note?

5. True or false: all melody notes identified as **chord notes** must be present in the selected chord.

6. True or false: the only way to end a cadence is with chord I or chord V.

Exercise 2: Suggest Suitable Chord Progressions and Cadences

Suggest suitable chord progressions for two cadences by indicating one chord (I, II, IV or V) at each of the places marked A-E. You do not have to indicate the position/inversion of the chords.
Show the chords by writing I, II etc.

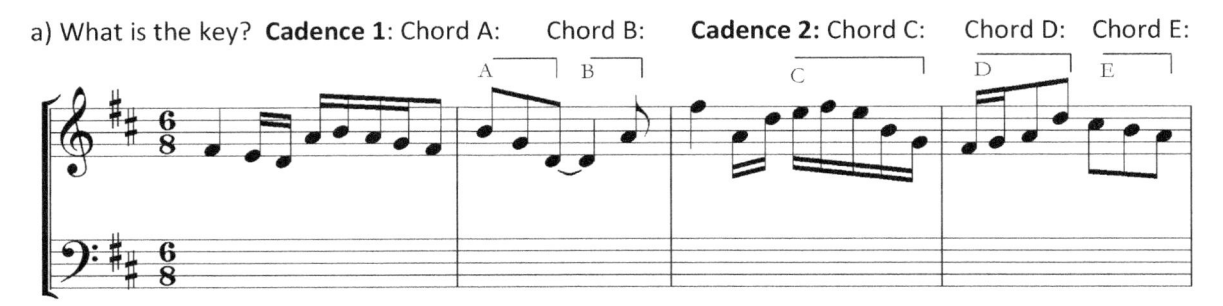

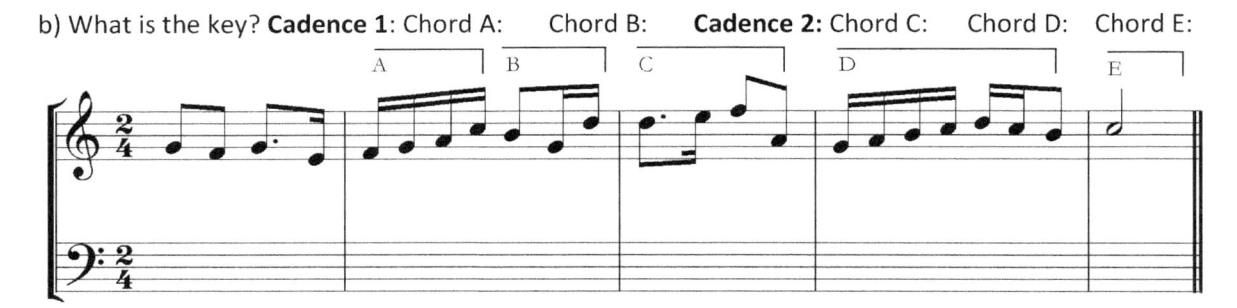

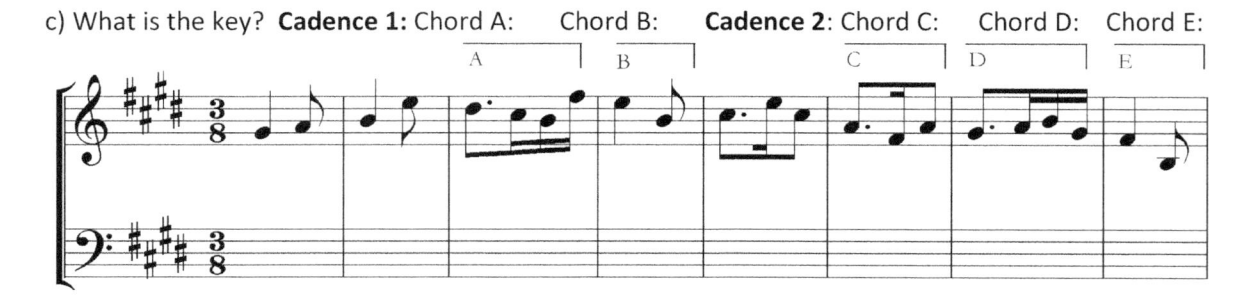

a) What is the key? **Cadence 1**: Chord A: Chord B: **Cadence 2**: Chord C: Chord D: Chord E:

b) What is the key? **Cadence 1**: Chord A: Chord B: **Cadence 2**: Chord C: Chord D: Chord E:

c) What is the key? **Cadence 1**: Chord A: Chord B: **Cadence 2**: Chord C: Chord D: Chord E:

Exercise 3: Name the Cadences

Describe each of the following cadences as **perfect**, **plagal**, or **imperfect**

a.

b.

c.

d.

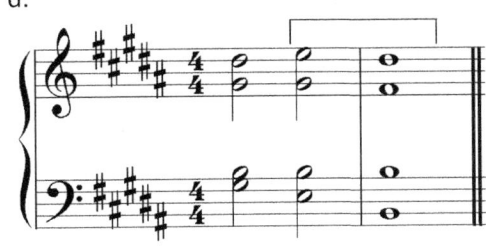

e.

PROGRESSIONS AND CADENCES ANSWERS

Exercise 1

1. A cadence is made up of two chords.

2. A progression is any sequence of changing chords. A cadence is two specific chords which mark the end of a section or piece of music.

3. V-I, IV-I, I-V, IV-V, II-V

4. A note which is an interval of a second (scale step) away from the last chord note is a non-chord note.

5. True: all melody notes identified as **chord notes** must be present in the selected chord.

6. True: the only way to end a cadence is with chord I or chord V.

Exercise 2

a. The key is D major

A: IV B: I C: II D: I E: V

b. The key is C major

A: IV B: V C: II D: V E: I

c. The key is E major

A: V B: I C: II D: I E: V

Exercise 3

a. imperfect   b. perfect   c. perfect   d. plagal   e. perfect

11. INSTRUMENTS

You need to know about all the **standard** orchestral instruments, and about the human voice.

You need to know which **family** each instrument belongs to, the relative **pitch** of each instrument and which **clef** they use.

You also need to know which instruments can play each other's music **without** a change in **pitch** occurring.

Families of Instruments

There are four families of instrument. Each family is defined by the way the instruments produce sound.

- Instruments which use strings are called **string** instruments (funnily enough!)
- Instruments which produce sound when they are hit or shaken are called **percussion**.
- Instruments which use air are divided into two groups - those that are always made of metal and which are played with a funnel-shaped mouthpiece are **brass** instruments, and those which can be made of wood are called **woodwind**.

Reed Instruments

In the woodwind family, the clarinet, oboe and bassoon all produce sound using a **reed**. The clarinet is a **single-reed** instrument, and the oboe and bassoon are **double-reed** instruments. A double reed is simply two reeds bound together at one end You may be asked about which are single- or double-reed instruments, so learn this!

Unpitched Instruments

The instruments in the strings, woodwind and brass families are all **pitched** instruments. This means they play notes which have a specific pitch, which you can write on a stave. In the percussion family, some instruments are pitched, and others are **unpitched**. Unpitched instruments make a "sound" but not a "note". Here are some examples.

Pitched Percussion

Xylophone (made of wood), glockenspiel (made of metal), timpani (or "kettle drums").

A kettle drum can only be tuned to play one note at a time, so usually you find two or three in an orchestra, each tuned to play different notes (e.g. the tonic and dominant).

Unpitched Percussion

Gong, triangle, cymbals, castanets, bass drum, snare drum.

Family Members of Instruments

Here's a table to summarise the standard orchestral instruments.

In each family the instruments are listed in order from the smallest (=highest) to the biggest (=lowest). You can see which clef the instruments normally use, and if they are transposing.

Family	Instrument		Clef	Transposing?
String	Violin	𝄞	Treble	No
	Viola	𝄡	Alto	No
	Cello	𝄢 𝄡 𝄞	Treble, tenor & bass	No
	Double bass	𝄢	Bass	8ve down
Woodwind	Flute	𝄞	Treble	No
	Oboe	𝄞	Treble	No
	Clarinet	𝄞	Treble	Yes (Bb/A)
	Bassoon	𝄢 𝄡 𝄞	Treble, tenor & bass	No
Brass	Trumpet	𝄞	Treble	Yes (Bb)
	French horn	𝄞	Treble	Yes (F)
	Trombone	𝄢 𝄡 𝄞	Treble, tenor & bass	No
	Tuba	𝄢	Bass	No

Non-Standard Instruments

There are plenty more instruments around as you probably know! They are not considered to be "standard" orchestral instruments though, because they are not used in a basic "standard" symphony orchestra.

Some examples include the guitar, the saxophone (pictured), the harp, the piano and the recorder.

Brass and woodwind instruments come in a variety of different sizes. A small flute is called a *piccolo*, whereas a big flute is called a *bass flute*. Clarinets come in many sizes too - you might have seen a small clarinet called an *E flat clarinet*, or a very big one which is a *bass clarinet*. A variant of the oboe is the *cor anglais*.

These instruments are often used in symphony orchestras, but they are not "standard" because they are used *in addition to* (and not normally *instead of*) the standard instruments. Many brass instruments are used mainly in brass bands, and not so often in symphony orchestras, for example, the cornet or the flugelhorn.

For Grade 5 Theory, you need only to know about the "standard" instruments, but you will not be penalised if you want to show off your knowledge! If you are asked "What is the highest member of the woodwind family?", you may answer "flute" (standard instrument), or "piccolo" (non-standard instrument).

However, you would **not** be right if you answered "recorder", because it is not used in symphony orchestras.

The Voice

There are four basic ranges of voice. Women's voices can be **soprano** (the highest voice) or **alto**, and men's voices can be **tenor** or **bass** (the lowest voice).

In between soprano and alto, there is another female voice called **mezzo-soprano**, and between tenor and bass there is another male voice which is called **baritone**.

Here is the complete range from highest to lowest:

Soprano - Mezzo Soprano - Alto - Tenor - Baritone - Bass

INSTRUMENTS EXERCISES

1. Underline **one** of the following instruments which could play a piece of flute music so that it sounds at the same pitch:

Trombone - Timpani - Violin - French Horn

2. Which family of instruments does the instrument you chose in question 1 belong to? State its lowest-sounding member.

Family _____ Lowest member _____

3. Underline **one** of the following instruments which could play a piece of clarinet music so that it sounds at the same pitch:

Tuba - Viola - Oboe - Trumpet

4. Which family of instruments does the instrument you chose in question 3 belong to? State its lowest-sounding member.

Family _____ Lowest member _____

5. Underline **one** of the following instruments which could play a piece of cello music so that it sounds at the same pitch:

Bassoon - Cymbals - Viola - Clarinet

6. Now name the family of standard orchestral instruments to which the instrument you have underlined belongs and state its highest-sounding member.

Family _____ Instrument _____

7. Write the instruments given below in the correct order from **lowest** to **highest**.

Trombone - Tuba - Trumpet - French Horn

8. Write the voices given below in the correct order from **lowest** to **highest**.

Alto - Bass - Mezzo soprano - Baritone - Tenor - Soprano

9. Name a standard orchestral instrument that normally uses the bass clef and state the family to which it belongs.

Instrument _____ Family _____

10. Name a standard orchestral instrument that normally uses the alto clef and state the family to which it belongs.

Instrument _____ Family _____

11. Name a standard orchestral instrument that normally uses the treble clef and state the family to which it belongs.

Instrument _____ Family _____

12. Name the highest sounding member of each family of instruments:

Woodwind _____ Strings _____ Brass _____

13. Name the lowest sounding member of each family of instruments:

Woodwind _____ Strings _____ Brass _____

14. Name two double-reed instruments found in the standard orchestra.

15. Which of these instruments is unpitched?

Xylophone - French Horn - Gong - Oboe

16. Complete the following statements:

- The clarinet is a member of the woodwind family of standard orchestral instruments.
- The member of that family next in pitch above the clarinet is the (1)_____ and it normally uses the (2)_____ clef.
- The string family is another family of standard orchestral instruments and its lowest-sounding member is the (3)_____.
- The member of the string family next in pitch above the cello is the (4)_____ and it normally uses the (5)_____ clef.

INSTRUMENTS ANSWERS

1. Violin

2. String family, double bass.

3. Trumpet

4. Brass family, tuba.

5. Bassoon

6. Woodwind family, flute (or piccolo)

7. Tuba – Trombone – French Horn – Trumpet

8. Bass – Baritone – Tenor – Alto – Mezzo soprano - Soprano

9. Bassoon (woodwind) OR trombone or tuba (brass) OR cello or double bass (strings)

10. Viola (strings)

11. Flute, clarinet or oboe (woodwind) OR trumpet or French horn (brass) OR violin (strings)

12. Woodwind: flute; Strings: violin; Brass: trumpet

13. Woodwind:bassoon; Strings: double bass; Brass: tuba

14. Oboe and bassoon

15. Gong

16.
- The clarinet is a member of the woodwind family of standard orchestral instruments.
- The member of that family next in pitch above the clarinet is the (1) oboe and it normally uses the (2) treble clef.
- The string family is another family of standard orchestral instruments and its lowest-sounding member is the (3) double bass.
- The member of the string family next in pitch above the cello is the (4) viola and it normally uses the (5) alto clef.

GRADE 5 MUSIC THEORY PRACTICE TEST

Exam time limit - 2 hours

(More practice tests in the ABRSM Online Format are available from https://payhip.com/b/LXfp)

QUESTION 1

The following extract, which begins on the first beat of the bar, requires a different time signature for each bar. Put in the three correct time signatures. (3 points)

QUESTION 2

Describe the chords marked A, B and C in the extract below as I, II, IV or V.

Also indicate whether the lowest note of the chord is the root (a), 3rd (b) or 5th (c).

The key is C minor. (3 points)

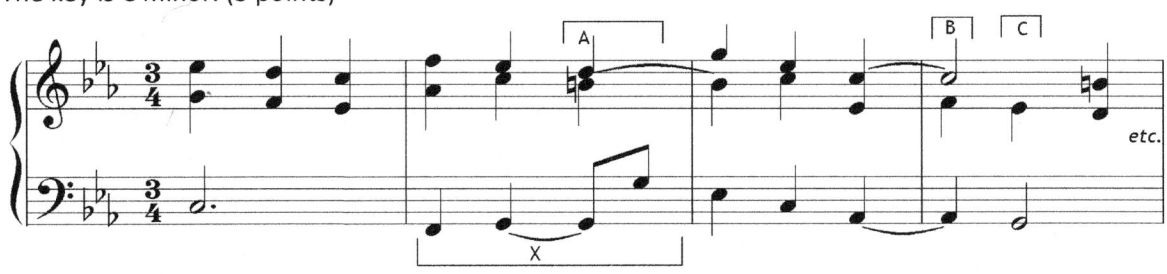

Chord A: __V a__   Chord B: __IV b__   Chord C: __I c__

QUESTION 3

Rewrite the left-hand part of bar 2 (question 2) (marked X) so that it sounds the same, but using the tenor clef. Remember to put in the key signature. (1 point)

QUESTION 4

Describe fully each of the numbered melodic intervals (e.g. major 2nd). (10 points)

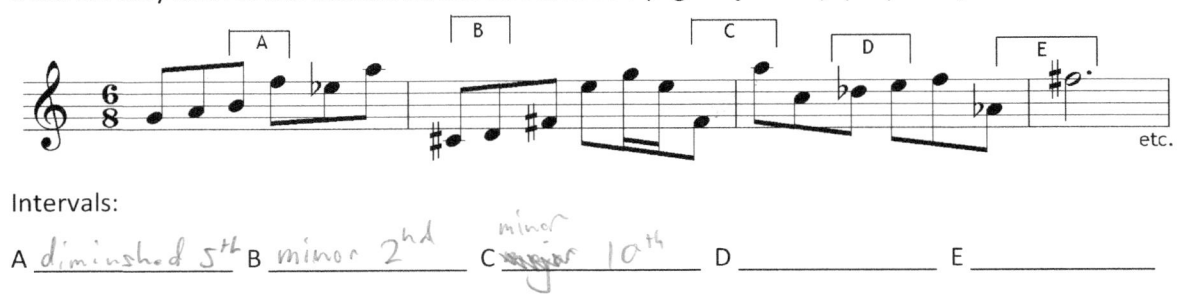

Intervals:

A diminished 5th   B minor 2nd   C minor 10th   D _____   E _____

QUESTION 5

This music is written for clarinet in A. Transpose it down a minor 3rd, as it will sound at concert pitch. Remember to put in the new key signature and add any necessary accidentals. (5 points)

QUESTION 6

a. Using semibreves (whole notes), write one octave ascending of the melodic minor scale that has this key signature. Begin on the tonic and remember to include any additional sharp, flat or natural signs. (5 points)

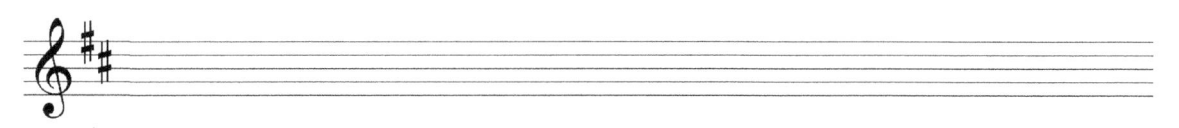

b. Choose the correct clef to make this into a **minor** scale. (1 point)

130

QUESTION 7

Look at this extract from a song, *Mit dem Grünen Lautenbande*, by Franz Schubert and then answer the questions that follow.

Give the meaning of:

a. *Mässig*. Choose from: A-Sadly | B-Moderately | C- Smoothly | D-Stately   (2 points)
b. 𝄐 (2 points) _____
c. 𝄇 (bar 2) (2 points) _____
d. 3 (bar 1) (2 points) _____
e. ⌒ (bar 10 left hand piano) (2 points) _____

131

f. Describe the time signature as: Simple or compound? Duple, triple or quadruple? (2 points)

_____

g. Add the correct rests to the left-hand piano part to complete bar 2. (2 points)

h. Give the technical name (e.g. tonic, dominant) of the voice note in bar 5 marked X. Remember that the key is B flat major.

_____ (2 points)

i. Describe fully (e.g. major 2nd) the bracketed harmonic interval marked Y in the right-hand piano part of bar 7.

_____ (2 points)

j. The dotted F in the left-hand piano part of bar 10 (marked Z) is worth _____ demisemiquavers (thirty-second notes) in total. (2 points)

k. This extract is from a song written for a tenor voice. Write the voices below in the correct order from lowest to highest. The first answer is given. (4 points)

Mezzo soprano - Bass - Alto - Baritone - Tenor - Soprano

Bass _____

l. Name a standard orchestral instrument that normally uses the treble clef and state the family to which it belongs. (4 points)

Instrument _____ Family _____

m. Now name the highest-sounding member of a **different** family of orchestral instruments. (2 points)

_____

QUESTION 8

Suggest suitable progressions for two cadences in the following melody by indicating ONLY ONE chord (I, II, IV or V) at each of the places marked A-E. You do not have to indicate the position of the chords, or to state which note is in the bass. (5 points)

Show the chords:

EITHER (a) by writing I, II, etc. or any other recognized symbols on the lines below;

(b) by writing notes on the staves.

FIRST CADENCE:

Chord A _____

Chord B _____

SECOND CADENCE:

Chord C _____

Chord D _____

Chord E _____

QUESTION 9

Look at the following score which is from a keyboard suite by J.S. Bach and answer the questions which follow.

a. Name the ornaments found in the right-hand keyboard part in bars 1 and 4. (4 points)
Bar 1:   Bar 4:

b. The key of the piece is F major. What other key shares the same key signature? (2 points)

c. Write as a breve (double whole note) an enharmonic equivalent of the note marked A in bar 3. (3 points)

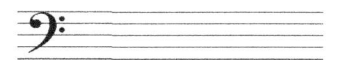

d. Rewrite the right-hand part of bar 1 using notes of **twice the value**. Include the new time signature. (4 points)

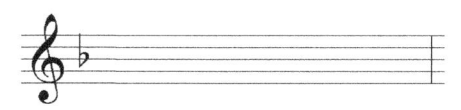

e. What is the technical name (e.g. tonic, dominant) of the highest note in the extract? Remember the key is F major. (2 points)

This page is blank.

PRACTICE TEST ANSWERS

The test is marked out of 100. A score of 66% is a pass, 80-89% is a merit, and 90%+ is a distinction.

QUESTION 1

QUESTION 2

A: Va   B: IVb   C: Ic

QUESTION 3

QUESTION 4

A: diminished 5th

B: minor 2nd

C: minor 10th or compound minor 3rd

D: augmented 2nd

E: augmented 6th

QUESTION 5

QUESTION 6

a.

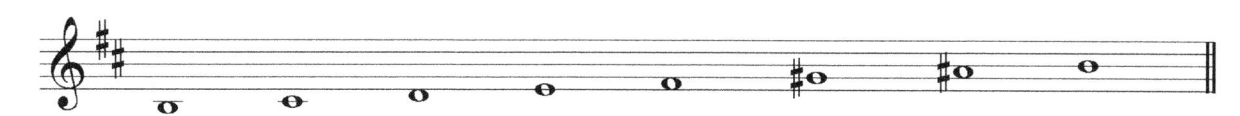

b.

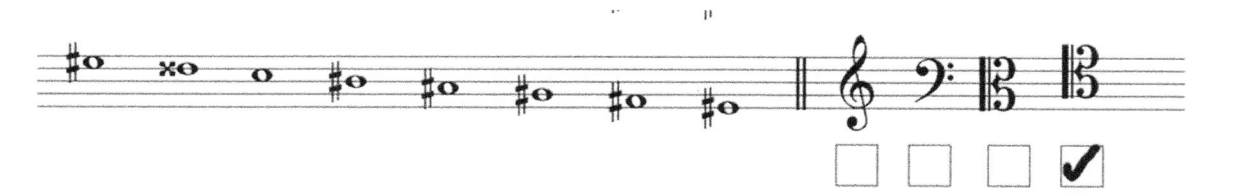

Question 7

a. B-Moderately
b. Pause
c. Repeat the following section
d. Triplet: play three notes in the time of two
e. Tie
f. Simple duple
g. [musical notation]

h. Mediant
i. Minor 6th
j. 7
k. (Bass) – Baritone – Tenor – Alto – Mezzo soprano – Soprano
l. Flute, oboe or clarinet (Woodwind) OR trumpet or French horn (Brass) OR violin (strings)
m. See (l)

Question 8

[musical notation with chord analysis: IV, I, II, I, V]

Question 9

a. Bar 1: Trill;   Bar 3: Upper mordent

b. D minor

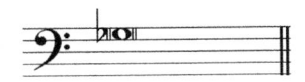

c. [musical notation]

d. [musical notation]

e. Supertonic

APPENDIX – SATB & COMPOSITION

The following sections on SATB and Composition were removed from the ABRSM syllabus from 1st January 2018. I have kept them in this appendix section for your reference, as they do contain useful information, especially if you are intending to continue to grade 6 (and I hope you are – it's worth it!)

SATB WRITING FOR VOICES
SATB

"SATB" is a quick way of referring to the four main voices that make up a choir, which are **Soprano**, **Alto**, **Tenor** and **Bass**.

Soprano and alto are women's voices, whereas tenor and bass are men's voices. Soprano is the highest voice and bass is the lowest.

OPEN SCORE AND SHORT SCORE

Vocal music for SATB is sometimes written on 4 staves with one for each voice, like this:

This is called "**open score**". The voices are always in this order: soprano (top), alto, tenor then bass (bottom).

The same music can also be written on two staves, with two voices on each stave, like this:

This is called "**short score**". Soprano and alto share the treble clef, and tenor and bass share the bass clef stave.

Open Score v. Short Score

Here are some of the main differences between open and short scores.

Clefs

In open score, the tenor voice uses a treble "octave" clef with a small 8 hanging off the tail:

This means that the music actually sounds an **octave lower** than written.

In short score, the tenor voice uses a **bass** clef.

Stems

In open score, the stems of the notes follow the shape of the melody.

In short score, soprano and tenor parts always have stems **up**, and alto and bass parts always have stems **down**.

We write: We **don't** write:

Ties

In open score, ties are always written on the opposite side of the note to the stem.

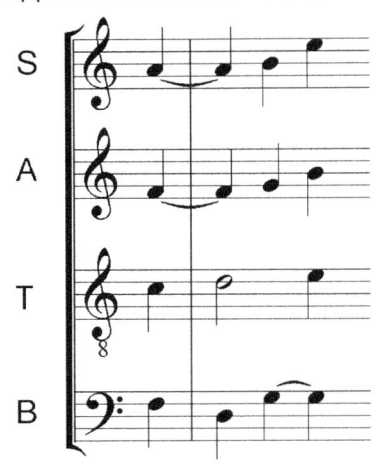

In short score, the ties on the soprano and tenor parts curve upwards, but the ties on the alto and bass parts always curve downwards.

Notice how the ties on the two soprano A's and the two bass G's have changed their shape:

Rests

In short score, rests are written near the **top** of the stave in the soprano and tenor parts, and near the **bottom** of the stave in the alto and bass parts. In open score, rests are placed in the **middle** of the stave.

Here are some rests written in short score. The soprano part begins with a quaver (eighth) rest, and the alto begins with a crotchet (quarter) rest.

Unisons and Seconds

Sometimes, two parts can sing an identical note or a "unison". In a short score, you need to show that the note belongs to **both** parts, and you do this by writing one note-head with two stems. One step points up, and the other points downwards.

Look at the soprano and alto parts in this open score: they are singing the same G.

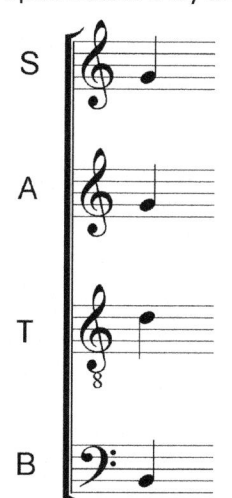

In short score, you will write one G, with two stems:

When two voices sing notes which are an interval of a 2nd apart, you won't be able to write them one above the other. Instead, you will need to move the **lower** note slightly to the **right** of the higher note, so that both can be clearly seen.

In this short score, the alto F needs to be moved slightly to the right, so that both notes can be seen:

If you try to align the G and F vertically, you will end up with an ugly blob like this!

How to Rewrite in Open Score

Let's try to rewrite these short score bars in open score.

141

1. Start by placing the clefs on each of the four staves, like this:

Don't forget the **little 8** on the tenor clef, and remember this means that the pitch of all the tenor notes is actually an octave **lower** than in the "normal" treble clef.

2. Copy the key signature and time signature onto **each** stave.

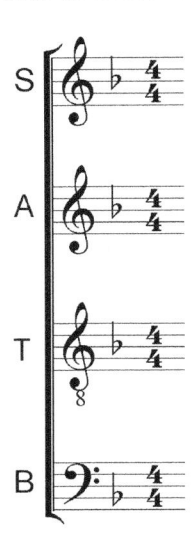

3. Copy the soprano, alto and bass lines note-for-note, but don't write the tenor line just yet.

Make sure you change the **stem direction** if necessary: remember that notes below the middle line have stems up, and notes above the middle line have stems down. Notes on the middle line follow the notes next to them.

Be sure to **line up the notes vertically** in exactly the same way as they are in the original.

This is the right way to do it: notice the stem direction and how the notes are aligned. The vertical line in the first bar shows how the notes line up correctly.

And this is the **wrong** way to do it! The lines show notes which should be in a straight line vertically, (because they sound at exactly the same time). The boxes show notes where the stems are pointing in the wrong direction.

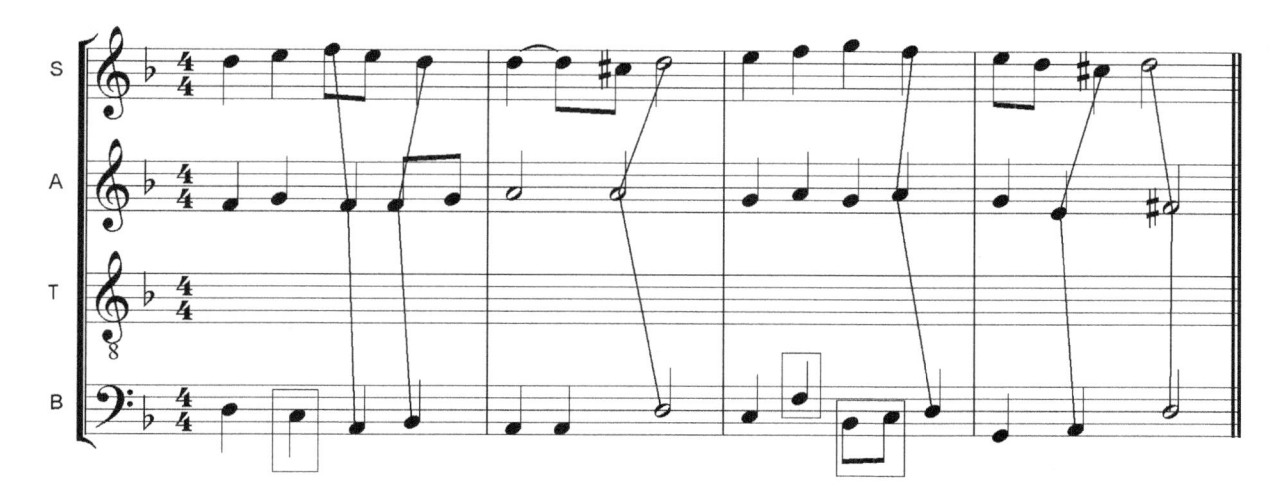

4. Now rewrite the tenor part in the **treble-octave clef**.

Remember that this clef sounds an octave **lower** than normal treble clef, so you will need to work out the exact pitch of the notes in the short score, then write them **up an octave in the open score**.

Middle C in bass clef is   but in treble-octave clef is

Make sure all the notes are aligned properly, and the stem directions are correct in the tenor part too.

Here is the finished re-writing:

5. Finally, make sure you've added any dots, ties and accidentals in the same way as in the original melody.

How to Rewrite in Short Score

Start by placing a treble and a bass clef, like this:

Copy the key signature and time signature onto each stave.

Using a ruler to keep the notes aligned vertically, copy the soprano, alto and bass lines, making sure that the **stem direction** is correct (soprano and tenor=up, alto and bass=down).

Rewrite the tenor part in bass clef. Remember where **middle** C lies!

Make sure you've added all dots, ties and accidentals.

SATB EXERCISES

Exercise 1: Rewriting in Short Score

a) This open score passage for SATB choir is adapted from Bach's Chorale No.362. Rewrite it in short score.

Exercise 1: Rewriting in Short Score

b) This open score passage is adapted from Bach's Fugue No.14 (Book 1 of the Well Tempered Klavier). Rewrite it in short score.

Exercise 2: Rewriting in Open Score

a) This short score passage for SATB choir is adapted from Bach's Chorale no. 300. Rewrite it in open score.

Exercise 2: Rewriting in Open Score

b) This passage is adapted from Bach's Fugue No.16 (Book 1 of the Well Tempered Klavier). Rewrite it in open score.

148

SATB ANSWERS

Exercise 1

Exercise 2

GENERAL COMPOSITION TIPS
COMPOSING MELODIES

This lesson looks at the **general** techniques needed for composing a short melody.

WRITING FOR AN INSTRUMENT (EXAMS BEFORE 2018)

You'll be given the first two bars of a melody, with the key and time signature. (It could be in treble clef or bass clef). The instructions will ask you to choose from two instruments and to continue writing the melody for the instrument you've chosen.

The choice of instruments will be from different families, for example the violin and oboe, or the bassoon and cello.

Here's an example question:

Compose a complete melody for unaccompanied violin or flute, using the given opening. Indicate the tempo and other performance directions, including any that might be particularly required for the instrument chosen. The complete melody should be eight bars long.

Instrument for which the melody is written: ....

WRITING FOR VOICE

You'll be given the first two lines of text, taken from poetry, and two blank staves. The instructions will ask you to write a **complete** melody for solo voice to fit the words of the text: you can choose whichever voice (soprano, alto, tenor or bass) you prefer.

You don't have to say which voice you've chosen, but you will have to keep the melody within the normal **range** of one voice, and use the appropriate **clefs**.

Here's an example question:

Compose a complete melody to the following words for a solo voice. Write each syllable under the note or notes to which it is to be sung. Also indicate the tempo and other performance directions as appropriate.

The river glares in the sun,   Like a torrent of molten glass.

Effective Composing

You might think that writing a melody without being able to hear it is impossible - but did you know that Beethoven wrote most of his great music when he was completely deaf?! Luckily, no one is asking you to write a 4-movement symphony - you only have to write a single melody line for 8 bars. But where do you start?

Every piece of music has two vital elements - **rhythm** and **melody**. On top of that, the **harmonic structure** of your composition will give shape to the melody, and should also be considered when composing. Also important are **performance directions**, which are words or symbols that help the musician interpret the notes they are reading. We'll look at each of these in turn.

Balance is also important: your melody should usually be 8 bars long, so you should break it down into two parts or "phrases". The first phrase will be bars 1-4, and the second phrase will be bars 5-8. If you like, you can then divide each phrase into 2, giving you four short 2-bar mini-phrases. We can call these four mini-phrases 1a, 1b, 2a and 2b.

Let's look at **rhythm, melody, harmonic structure and performance directions** in more detail.

(These examples are based on an 8-bar melody. If you choose the voice question, you can write it for as many bars as you think appropriate, but eight is an **excellent** choice, because it is the most balanced. If you don't choose eight bars, then write it for four. Don't choose any other number!)

Rhythm

I want you to forget about melody for now, so in the following examples I'm going to use a one-line stave, so that we can focus on rhythm only.

Here are the opening bars (phrase 1a and 1b) of some well-known tunes, notated in rhythm only:

1. British National Anthem:

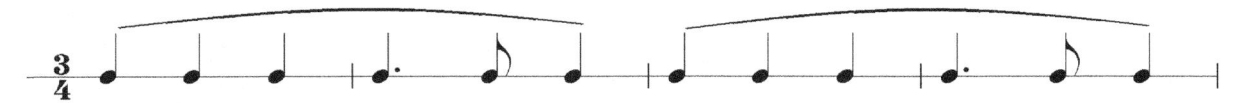

2. Beethoven Symphony no.5, 1st movement

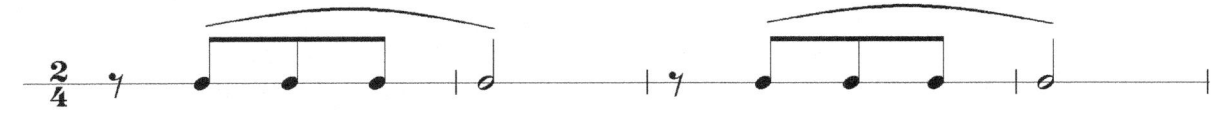

3. Happy Birthday to You/Star Spangled Banner

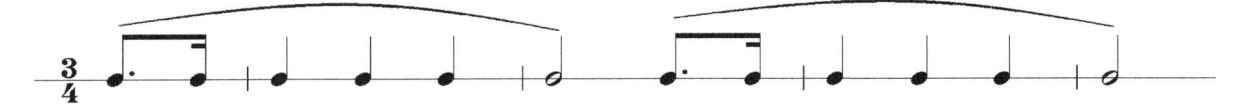

What do they all have in common?

They each have a rhythmic **phrase** which is **repeated** to create phrase 1b.

You **shouldn't** write your second phrase with **exactly** the same rhythm as the first (because your composition will be too short), but it must be quite **similar**.

Look at how I've altered the second phrase of those three extracts, (tap out the rhythms on the table as you read them!)

1.

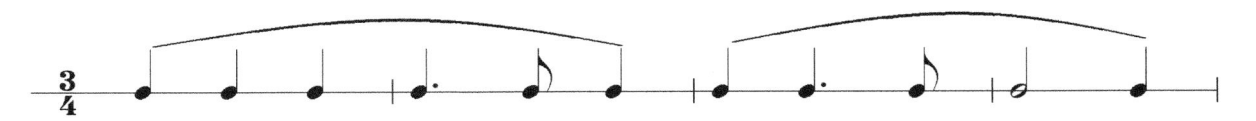

2.

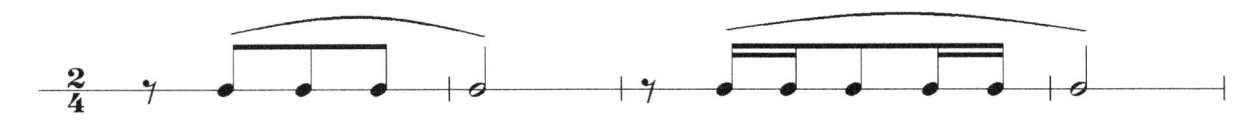

3.

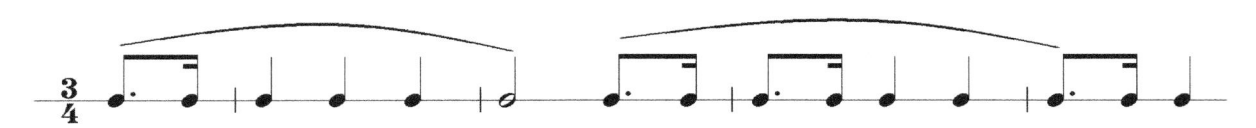

What kind of changes did I make?

Extract 1: I swapped around the rhythm from bar 2 to make bar 3, and used an extended note value in bar 4.

Extract 2: I changed a quaver (8th note) into 2 semiquavers (16th notes) in two places.

Extract 3: I reused the dotted quaver/semiquaver (dotted 8th/16th) pattern to make a livelier second phrase.

You can change the rhythm of phrase 1a in any number of ways; the important thing is **not** to change it **too much**!

The same guidelines apply when you create phrases 2a and 2b - keep the rhythms similar, but make small changes, and make sure that phrase 2 is not identical to phrase 1.

There are not many rules about how you should adapt the rhythm, except that there must be some **connection** and some **similarity** between the rhythms - don't write a completely different rhythm for each of your four phrases, and it must not be too **repetitive**.

WRITING RHYTHMS

When you write your composition, be sure to use rhythms and groupings which are correct for the time signature. The rhythms used in 3/4 are not the same as those used in 6/8, for example! Read the lesson on time signatures again, if necessary.

If the composition starts with an upbeat (or "anacrusis" or "pick-up"), the last bar of the melody needs to make up for it. Bar 1 is always the **first complete bar.**

For example, if you have a crotchet (quarter note) up beat in 3/4 time, then bar 8 will contain only **two crotchets (quarter notes)**, because the first and last bars added together total one complete bar.

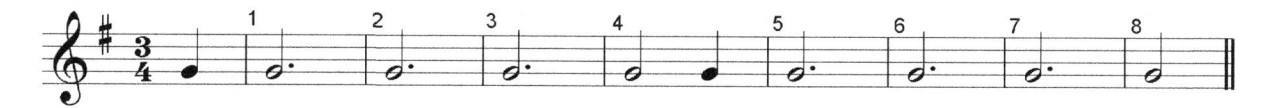

Here, for example, the first note is an upbeat. The last bar and the up beat bar added together make up a whole bar.

You don't need to add bar numbers, but you might find it useful to do so.

Only the first and last bars can be "incomplete". You will probably need to use two staves to write your whole composition out, so make sure the first bar on the second stave is **complete**: don't split a bar across two staves.

Don't forget to finish with a double bar line!

MELODY

Just like rhythms, melodies sound good if they contain repeated **sequences**. Do you know this children's song? (It's called *Frère Jacques*.)

This song simply repeats both the rhythm and melody in bars 1 and 3 to create bars 2 and 4.

But if you look more closely, you'll see that the melody in 1b (E-F-G) is the same as the first three notes of the melody in 1a (C-D-E), but a third higher. In both cases, the melody rises twice by a step.

This is an example of a **melodic sequence**: a section of melody which is repeated but starting on a different step of the scale.

However, *Frère Jacques* is probably not the most interesting song in the world, so let's look at another example!

This is the "Gloria" chorus from the Christmas carol *Ding Dong Merrily on High!*

The rhythm of each bar is the same, but the melody is in sequences, with each bar starting **one step down** in the key of G major, starting on the dominant note (D), then C (bar 2) then B (bar 3), then A (bar 4).

There are several types of sequence which you can use to generate new melodic phrases, so let's look at them in more detail.

SEQUENCES

This is the bar we're going to sequence.

Type of Sequence	Example	Notes
Melodic Sequence Change the starting note but keep all the relative intervals the same:		This sequence starts a 2nd higher.
		This one starts a 5th higher.
Inversion Turn the melody upside down:		
Retrograde Write the melody back to front:		
Retrograde Inversion Upside down **and** back to front:		

You can also combine any of the above types of sequence.

Your new melody should be a **mix** of your own ideas and some imitation of what's already there - your new ideas need to be **linked** to the two bars you've already been given. Be inventive, but don't stray too far away!

(By the way, don't worry about remembering all the names of the different types of sequences; you won't be tested on them!)

In the instrumental question, you are given an opening to adapt in order to create the rest of the composition. In the vocal question, you will have to invent **your own opening**, but you will then need to adapt it to create the rest of the melody.

Harmonic Structure

(See Lesson 10 for basic information about progressions and cadences.)

Although you are only writing one line of music, you should keep in mind the chords that could accompany your melody.

Your piece should be constructed in two halves of exactly the same length. At the end of each half, you need to use notes which fit an appropriate **cadence.**

- In a short, 8-bar tune, the end of the first phrase sounds best if it ends on an **imperfect cadence**. This means that the end of the phrase sounds good if it is played with chord **V**. The chord before **V** is up to you, but common imperfect cadences are **I-V, II-V, IV-V** and **VI-V**. Make sure that the notes which end your first phrase fit into one of these cadence chords.

- The end of the second phrase should end with a **perfect** cadence: **V-I**. Always end your composition with a **tonic** note, with the value of at least a crotchet (quarter note).

Make sure the notes you have chosen for your melody **fit** the cadences at these points. (Don't forget that your non-chord notes don't count). Make the last chord of each cadence fall on the first beat of the bar – bar 4 for the imperfect cadence, and bar 8 for the final perfect cadence.

For the rest of your piece, it will sound great if your **harmonic structure** is good. Each bar of your composition should fit with a chord which exists in the key of your piece. (Work out which are chord notes and non-chord notes in exactly the same way as you do when working out cadences.)

A good harmonic structure is one which uses:

- Chords I, IV and V at least half of the time
- Chords II and VI occasionally
- A different chord on each beat, or in each bar. Don't use the same harmony for more than one bar's worth: keep it moving.

Use chords I and V at the start of a composition. In the instrument composition, you'll be given the opening, so you don't need to worry about this. But if you choose the vocal composition, remember to use I and V straight away.

Chord III is not used very often, and is probably best avoided. Chord VII works the same way as chord V, because it fools our ears into thinking it is V7 (V with an added 7th e.g. G-B-D-F in the key of C major).

In a minor key, you need to base your chords on the **harmonic** minor scale. This means that chord V is always a major chord (e.g. E major in the key of A minor). Chord III must be avoided (because it is C-E-G# (for example, in A minor), which is an **augmented** chord, which is nasty). Chord VII also uses the raised leading note in a minor key (e.g. G#-B-D in A minor).

Here's a summary of the **recommended chords** to use in a major and minor key:

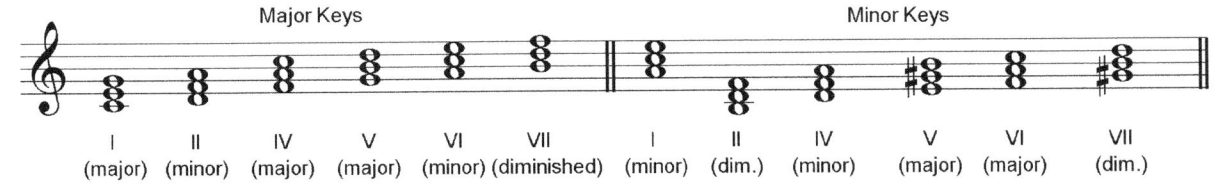

Major Keys | Minor Keys

I	II	IV	V	VI	VII	I	II	IV	V	VI	VII
(major)	(minor)	(major)	(major)	(minor)	(diminished)	(minor)	(dim.)	(minor)	(major)	(major)	(dim.)

Here is an example of a composition with a strong harmonic structure. The key is B minor.

The melody begins with chords I and V, the first phrase ends with an imperfect (IV-V) cadence, with chord V falling on the first beat of bar 4. The end of the piece uses a perfect (V-I) cadence, with chord I falling on the first beat of bar 8.

The rest of the piece mainly uses chords I, IV and V, with II and VI also used occasionally. Non-chord notes are marked with an X (remember, non-chord notes are an interval of a 2nd away from the previous chord note: see the lesson on progressions for more info.)

The harmony changes at least every bar, sometimes it changes with each beat of the bar (e.g. bar 5).

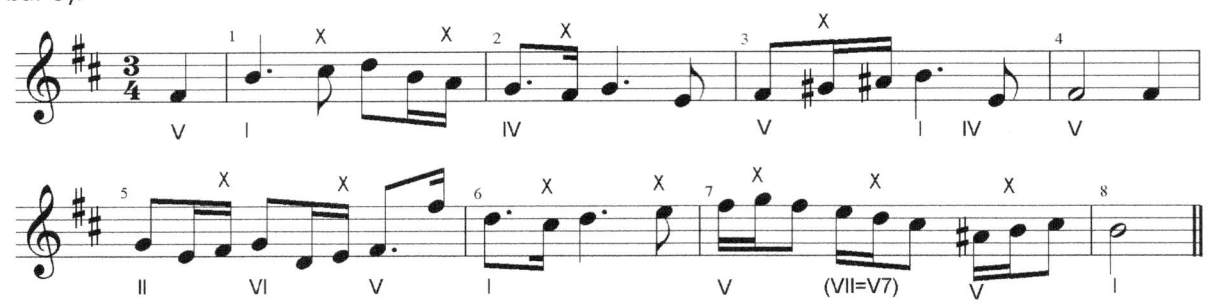

Performance Directions

Whatever instrument/voice you're writing for, you will need to include performance directions for the player/singer.

You **must** include:

Tempo (speed)

- Use an accepted Italian, German or French musical terms. You won't get extra marks for using an obscure term, so it's a good idea to play it safe and use a common term such as "Moderato". Write the tempo **above** the first note.

- If you pick a very fast or very slow tempo, you might make the composition quite awkward to play for a particular instrument, so unless you are 100% sure, use "Moderato" or "Andante", which are both moderate tempos.

- You can use a metronome marking if you prefer, but be sure to use a number which is actually found on a metronome (you couldn't use the number 59, for example!) Also, make sure you use the value of note which is indicated by the time signature. If the time signature is 4/4, you would use a crotchet (quarter note), because the time signature means "count crotchet (quarter notes)". If the time signature is 6/8 though, you would have to use a dotted crotchet (dotted quarter note), because 6/8 is a compound time signature.

Dynamics (volume)

- The player/singer needs to know what dynamic the piece begins at, so add a starting dynamic (e.g. "mf"), directly **under** the first note for instruments, or **above** it for voices.

- You should also indicate some gradual increases/decreases of volume with hairpins e.g. ───────. Make sure that the beginning and end of the hairpin is accurately placed under specific notes. Line up the hairpins under a specific starting and ending note.

- Make sure that all the dynamics you write are logical. If you write "mp < pp" it is very confusing, since you have indicated a crescendo which gets quieter!

- It's a good idea to make the loudest part of the melody happen somewhere around bars 6-8, as this is where we expect to hear a musical climax.

TOP TIPS

My best tip is to keep in your mind that a little goes a long way. Adapt the opening melody without changing it drastically add just a few performance directions to the player - but be sparing.

Take a look at some of the music you're playing right now- just how many directions can you find in the space of 8 bars? Not many, I'd guess!

If you try to write something very complicated, you're more likely to get into a mess. Keep it clean and simple, but make sure you do add **some** directions, which are both **relevant** and **meaningful**.

HOW CAN I LEARN TO HEAR MY COMPOSITIONS IN MY HEAD?

Get into the **habit** of hearing music in your head. You'll find this question much easier if you can accurately pinpoint the notes you're writing, (you won't be able to sing them out loud in the exam room!)

Everyone can hear music in their head (sometimes you get a tune going round and round in there that you can't get rid of), but learning to hear in your head what your **eyes** are seeing is a little harder. Take some music which you haven't studied yet and try to **read it without playing/singing it**. Don't panic - the more you practise, the easier it will get.

Start off with just 2-4 bars, and build it up as you become more confident. Choose music that moves in small steps, not in big intervals, and without lots of accidentals. Check what was in your head by playing the bars on your instrument. Were they the same?

Gradually move on to more complicated music- with difficult key signatures, tricky rhythms and huge leaps. Learning the skill of hearing music in your head also helps your sight-reading a lot!

You might find it easier if you make some kind of physical reaction as you read - if you can sing, you might feel your voice-box subconsciously changing as you change notes; if you play an instrument it might help if let your fingers move on an imaginary instrument.

Composer's Checklist

Here's a checklist to use while you're doing practice questions. (See Lessons 13 and 14 for more details).

All	Tempo	
	Dynamics	
	Phrasing	
	Double bar at end	
	Range of notes fits	
	Cadences (1st=?-V, 2nd=V-I)	
	Sequences	
	Long tonic note at end	
Wind Instruments	Articulation	
	Range fits the instrument	
String Instruments	Articulation	
	Range fits the instrument	
Voice	Breathing (phrasing)	
	Clef, Key and Time	
	Syllables ok	
	Word Painting	
	Style consistent	

GENERAL COMPOSITION EXERCISES

- This unit contains a few exercises to test your understanding of how to tackle the composition question in the grade 5 music theory exam.
- Exam style questions can be found in the following lessons.

EXERCISE 1 - GENERAL KNOWLEDGE ABOUT COMPOSITIONS

1. Which of these is the ideal number of bars for a vocal composition in the grade 5 theory exam: 5 bars, 7 bars, 8 bars, 10 bars?

2. On which note of the scale should a composition end (give its technical name)?

3. Which of these note values is ideal as the final note of a composition: minim (half note), quaver (8th note), semiquaver (16th note)?

4. Which of these are essential to add to your melody: tempo, dynamics, articulation (e.g. slurs)?

5. True or False: In order to get top marks in the composition question, you need to show a great deal of imagination and creativity.

6. If there is an upbeat (or "anacrusis" or "pick up"), which bar do you count as bar 1?

EXERCISE 2 - ADAPTING AN OPENING

Find the odd one out: which one bar would **NOT** be suitable to use in the same composition as the given bar? Give reasons for your choices.

a. Given bar:

Which bar wouldn't fit?

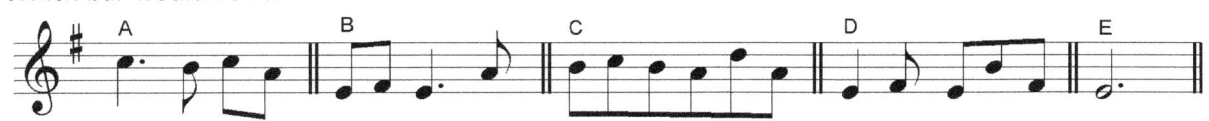

b. Given bar:

Which bar wouldn't fit?

GENERAL COMPOSITION ANSWERS

Exercise 1

1. 8 bars is the ideal length.

2. A composition should end on the tonic (keynote).

3. A minim (half note).

4. All of them.

5. False: In order to get top marks in the composition question, you DO NOT need to show a great deal of imagination and creativity. You need to write a balanced, coherent melody, with a good harmonic foundation and appropriate performance directions.

6. If there is an upbeat (or "anacrusis" or "pick up"), bar 1 is the first complete bar.

Exercise 2

a)

A fits, because it's a melodic sequence of the given bar.

B fits, because it's a nearly exact inverted sequence of the given bar.

C fits, because it's based on the interval movement on the given bar, which moves by 2nds and a 4th.

D **doesn't fit**, because the rhythm is written in 6/8 time, with the quavers (8th notes) grouped to add up to a dotted crotchet (dotted quarter note). In 3/4 time, all four quavers (8th notes) should be beamed together.

E fits, because it would be fine as the last note of the composition.

b)

A **doesn't fit**, because most of the intervals used (4ths and a compound 2nd) don't occur in the given bar, and the rhythm is completely different.

B fits, because the first group of notes is built on rising 3rds like the given bar, and the rhythm of the second group of notes is the same as the given bar.

C fits, because the rhythms are the same but the two halves of the bar have been swapped, and the melody is built from 3rds in the second half of the bar.

D fits, because the first half is built on 3rds like the given bar, and the second half rises a 2nd from F to G (first to the last note) in the same way as the given bar rises from Bb to C.

COMPOSING A MELODY FOR INSTRUMENTS (EXAMS BEFORE 2018)

THE GRADE FIVE MUSIC THEORY INSTRUMENTAL COMPOSITION QUESTION

In your exam, you'll be given the first two bars of a melody, with the key and time signatures. (It could be in treble clef or bass clef.)

The instructions will ask you to choose from two instruments and to continue writing the melody for the instrument you've chosen. (There is no wrong answer- choose the instrument you are most comfortable with).

The choice of instruments will be from different orchestral families, for example the violin and oboe, or the bassoon and cello.

You will never have to write for an instrument on which we usually play several notes at the same time, like the piano, harp or organ.

Here's an example question:

Compose a melody for solo violin or oboe, using the given opening. Include tempo and other performance directions, and any that might be specially needed for the instrument you've chosen. The finished melody should be eight bars long.

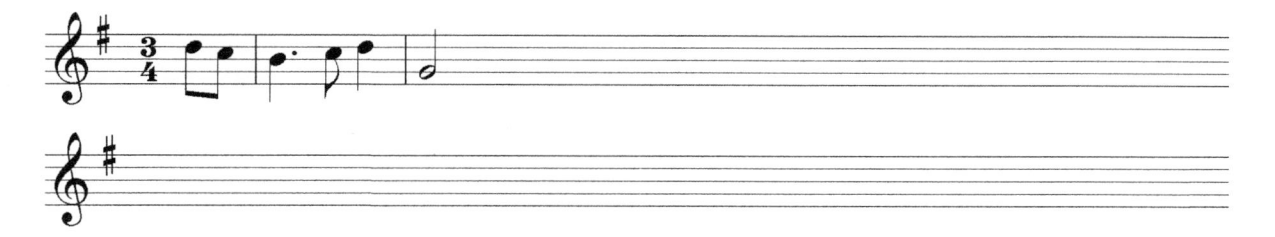

CHOOSING AN INSTRUMENT

It's a good idea to choose an instrument that you know something about! If you play the clarinet and you have the choice of bassoon or cello, you'll probably write a better melody for the bassoon, as it is also a wind instrument. Whichever instrument you choose, you will need to know its **range**, i.e. what its lowest and highest notes are.

As long as you don't start using lots of ledger lines you should stay within the range required, but don't forget that some instruments are less/more effective in different registers. For example, although the flute can play from middle C, the very lowest notes are quite weak and much less bright than octave above.

Don't forget to write which instrument you have chosen on your exam paper!

Melody Length

The melody should be exactly 8 bars in total. You usually get around 2 bars to start you off, so you will have to write 6.

Notice whether the melody starts with a **complete** bar or not - if it starts with an incomplete bar, then your last bar should make up the beats, (so you'll finish up with 7 complete bars and 2 incomplete bars). Bar 1 is the first **complete** bar.

Performance Directions

Don't forget you must include tempo and dynamics (see the previous lesson). When writing for an instrument, you must also include **articulation** directions.

Articulation (attack)

Adding the right articulation indications will increase the marks you get for this question - but make sure you use them in the right places and don't overdo it.

- If there are no articulation markings, a wind player (woodwind and brass) has to attack each and every note with the tongue, and a string player has to change the bow direction with every note. This is not only tiring for the player, but it makes the music sound rather jagged and unlyrical.

- The **legato** marking (or "slur") is used to show that wind players should play a group of notes with one breath, or that string players should play a group of notes with one sweep of the bow. Be sure to use legato markings in your composition.
  You can slur all the notes in one bar, or half bars, or groups of faster notes, like quavers.
  Don't slur more than one bar though - a wind player is likely to run out of breath, and a string player will run out of bow!
  Slurs should be written on the opposite side of the note to the stem, but it's ok to write them on the other side if there isn't enough space.
  Here are some different ways you could slur the same melody, slurring the whole bar, the half bar, and the pairs of quick notes:

- You can also use other types of articulation, such as staccato, accents and tenuto, but these are optional.

- Whatever articulation you use, try to be **consistent** throughout the melody. For example, you slurred each half bar from bars 1-4, then you should do the same in bars 5-8. If you put staccato on the semiquavers (16th notes) in bar 2 (for example), then do the same for any similar notes/rhythms in the rest of the piece.

Tempo, dynamics and articulation are the only performance directions that you **must** add. There are some other markings which are optional:

Breathing

Wind players will need somewhere to breathe. You may indicate places where the player can grab a quick intake of air by using a small comma - above the stave.

Although you don't have to put breathing marks in, you do have to make sure that your melody is playable by a human player! If you slurred all the notes across four bars and put a tempo of "*molto adagio*", you would end up with a dead flautist. Think about what you are writing!

Pauses

It can be nice to add a pause symbol on the last note of your piece.

Bowing Directions

String parts sometimes include special symbols which tell the player whether to play a note with their bow moving upwards or downwards.

However, bowing directions are normally only used a) in beginner's study books to help them out or b) when the direction of the bow is not what the string player would expect.

What does a string player expect? A "down bow" is used on a "down beat". A "down beat" is another word for a strong beat; the first beat of a bar is always a "down beat". (It gets this name because a conductor moves his/her hand downwards to show the first beat of each bar). An "upbeat" occurs before or after a down beat, and the player uses an "up bow". So, if your composition begins with an upbeat (or "anacrusis" or "pick up"), then a competent string player would automatically play it with an "up bow" and then use a "down bow" for the first beat of bar 1, and so on.

For this reason, it's completely unnecessary to cover your 8-bar string melody with bowing directions. You won't get extra marks for them, and you might end up losing marks if they don't make logical sense.

If, on the other hand, you happen to be an advanced string player and are confident that you know how to use bowing directions for good effect, then by all means use them.

Special Effects

String instruments are capable of playing more than one note at the same time (this is called "double-stopping"). A whole range of sounds can be produced by striking the strings in different ways, such as "pizzicato" (plucking the strings with the fingers), "tremolo" (shimmering the bow rapidly up and down) or "spiccato" (using the wooden part of the bow instead of the hairy part).

Wind instruments can produce effects such as "flutter-tonguing", double and triple tonguing, glissandos (slides between notes) and so on.

Both wind and string instruments can play "vibrato", and brass/string instruments can play with a mute.

None of these special effects are necessary for your exam composition, and we would strongly recommend **avoiding** them.

The examiner is not looking for fireworks: they are looking for a balanced, well-constructed composition.

COMPOSING A MELODY FOR INSTRUMENTS EXERCISES

Write 8-bar compositions using the given openings. State which instrument you have chosen. Add performance directions throughout.

Violin or clarinet

Bassoon or trombone

COMPOSING A MELODY FOR VOICE (EXAMS BEFORE 2018)

The Voice Composition Question

In the Grade 5 Theory voice composition question you'll be given two lines of text, usually taken from poetry, and two blank staves.

The instructions will ask you to write a **complete** melody for solo voice to fit the words of the text: you can choose whichever voice (soprano, alto, tenor or bass) you prefer.

You don't have to write which voice you've chosen, but you will have to keep the melody within the normal **range** of one voice. You can use either the treble or bass clef, whichever you are more comfortable with.

Try to avoid extreme highs and lows of the range.

Melody Length

The length of the melody is up to you, but a well-balanced melody will normally last for **4** or **8** complete bars: each line of text should fit into 2 or 4 bars.

Often the melody will **need** to start with an upbeat (which means an incomplete bar), in which case the last bar should make up the missing beats. Don't forget to finish on the tonic note, with a double bar line! (Reasons why your melody might **need** to start with an upbeat are explained below).

Writing the Melody

The voice composition question is assessed in quite a few different ways. You will need to work out a rhythm which fits the **stress** of the words, and a melody which suits the **meaning** of the words. It's a good idea to begin by sorting out the rhythm, then add a melody to the rhythm when you've worked it out.

Each individual syllable of the text needs to be set to at least one note. To make a good rhythm, you need to work out where the **stressed syllables** are in the given words, and place the stressed syllables on the **strong beats of the bar.**

Then you need to pick a suitable time signature and construct the entire rhythm of the piece. Next, you need to decide on the mood of the piece (based on the meaning of the words), and create a melody which fits the rhythm and mood.

Finally, you should add performance directions to your composition.

Write in the words as you write each musical note, so that you have enough space for both. When you have finished, check that the way the words are written for each note has been done correctly - this is known as the "verbal underlay" (explained below!) If you write all the melody first, you'll find that you haven't got enough space to write the words neatly. If you write all the text first, you will probably get the relative spacing of the notes wrong!

So here are the steps:

1. Work out the stressed syllables
2. Choose a time signature and write a rhythm
3. Choose a mood and key, and write the melody/words underneath
4. Add performance directions
5. Check the verbal underlay

1. Work out the stressed syllables

Look at your first line of text and decide which syllables you think should be **stressed** - these words will be sung naturally on the first beat of the bar.

How easy this is depends on the words you've got. Here are some examples.

Old castles on the cliffs arise,

Proudly towering in the skies.

Here are the stressed syllables underlined:

Old <u>cas</u>tles on the <u>cliffs</u> arise,

<u>Proud</u>ly towering <u>in</u> the skies.

How did I work out the stresses?

Try saying the words aloud and clapping or tapping your foot in time. If you seem to be clapping on every word, try clapping at **half** the speed (but carry on speaking at the same speed). Say the lines aloud several times without stopping, and you should start to instinctively start clapping on **four** accented words.

(If you find this very difficult to do, you should probably choose the question on writing for an instrument, rather than for voice.)

Here's another example, which is a bit harder:

The river glares in the sun

Like a torrent of molten glass

Try the same clapping exercise. Again, halve the speed of your clapping if you seem to be clapping all the time. You should end up clapping at these points:

The <u>ri</u>ver glares in the <u>sun</u>

Like a <u>tor</u>rent of molten <u>glass</u>

2. Write the rhythm

Now take your pencil again, and sketch in a rhythm above each line of text. You can either choose a time signature before you start, or "see how it goes" and select one at the end.

Most texts will fit into a variety of time signatures, and there isn't one single correct answer. However, sometimes the words of the text might lead you to choose a particular time signature; for example, words about a battle could suggest a marching 2/4, or romantic words often sound smoother in triple time.

Be consistent: use similar types of rhythms throughout. Don't be too repetitive though, and make sure that the first and second halves of the piece are similar but not identical. (They should be like fraternal (not identical) twins: with some similarities, but easy to see the differences!)

You need to write at least one note value per syllable. Feel free to write more than one note per syllable if you want!

Here are two possible rhythms for this text:

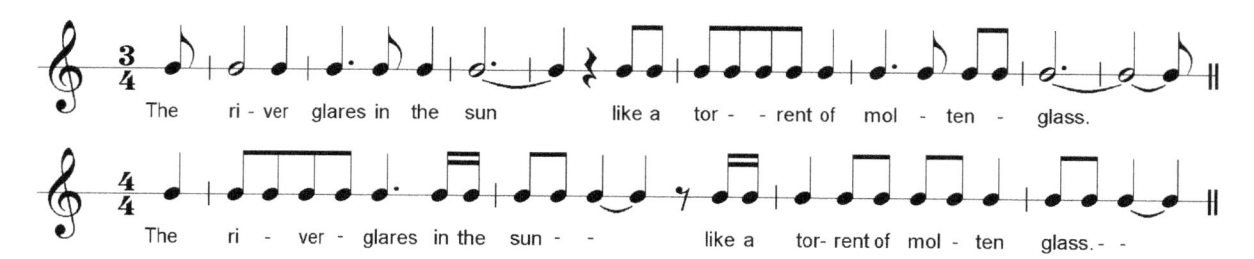

3. Mood and Melody

Decide whether the music should be in a **major** or **minor** key. Look at the words again and think about how they make you feel. If they are sunny, positive words, use a major key. If they are dark, sad or aggressive, use a minor key.

The words might also suggest a particular **style** to you. It could be a lullaby, a march, a love song or something else completely.

Think about **word painting**. Word painting is the technique of using notes to imitate the literal meaning of words in the text.

For example, if you have the word "low", you use a low note, if you have the words "soaring" you write ascending high notes and so on. Other evocative words could be "climb", "fall", "sigh", "stop," "rushing" and "jump". There won't always be words which you can paint with, but if you can find one, do try to use it!

4. Performance Directions

You will need to add a tempo at the beginning of the piece - again, think about the mood you want to create. You also need to add dynamics. You need a dynamic for the first note, and then some changes of dynamic which follow the mood and contours of the piece. Bear in mind that it is most natural to crescendo while singing a rising melody, and decrescendo when the melody falls.

It's a good idea to write any dynamics **above** the stave, so that they don't get mixed up with the words of the text.

5. Check the Verbal Underlay

Each syllable of the text must be aligned correctly, underneath its corresponding note.

When a word has **two or more syllables**, you need to break it up. Use **hyphens** (-) to link the syllables together. Break up the word so that each syllable starts with a consonant which you can sing. For example, let's break up the word "Constantinople". It's got five syllables, so the correct way to break it up is like this:

Con - stan - ti - no - ple

Each new syllable starts with a consonant which you can sing.

Here are two other ways to break it up, but they are **wrong**:

Co - nsta - nti - nop - le

This is wrong because you can't sing "nsta" or "nti", and "le" isn't pronounced that way in the word.

Cons - tant - i - no - ple

This is wrong because the "st" sound should be kept together, and the third syllable should start with a consonant.

Words that have grammatical endings such as "-ing" or "-ed" or "est" etc., can be split so that the main word is joined to its ending, for example "breath-ing" (not "brea-thing").

Here's a notated example of some hyphenated words:

Hap - py   birth - day   to   you

You can write **more than one** note to be sung to **one** syllable. Use one or more long **dashes** under each note that the syllable should be sung to, and connect the notes together with a **slur**, like the word "us" here:

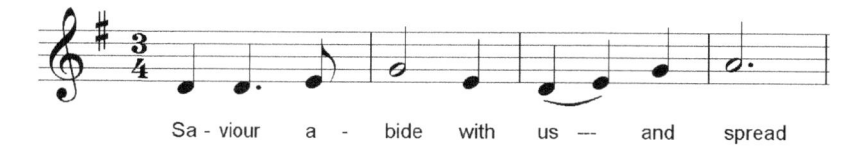

Sa - viour   a - bide   with   us ---   and   spread

BEAMING

In the old days, quavers and smaller were **not** supposed to be beamed together in vocal music. For separate syllables, you were supposed to write

and not

These days though, it's preferable to beam the notes together. You may well come across old vocal scores which use this old notation style. If you do, look more closely and see if you can identify any other changes in the way music is now written down!

BREATHING

Don't forget that singers need to breathe, especially if your tempo is slow! You don't need to notate breathing points, but keep in mind that it's easier to grab a quick breath at the end of a minim (half note) than in between quavers (8th notes)!

EXAMPLE COMPOSITION

Here's an example of a complete composition to the text "The river glares in the sun".

I chose the time signature of 3/4 because I feel that triple time feels more flowing and therefore more "river-like". I decided to make the word "river" meander around a bit in bar 5, whereas the word "glass" would be flat and still (word painting). Notice that the word "glass" doesn't need a hyphen - it's sung to a tied note, which counts as just one note.

I chose a minor key overall, because the words seem quite negative. However, I decided to write an imperfect cadence on the word "sun" in the relative major key (the notes fit the chords of G major then D major), because the word "sun" is positive. The key moves back to E minor at the end, with a perfect cadence on the syllables "-ten" and "glass" (chords of B major and E minor).

The melody begins low and gradually rises up to high E. For this reason, I started at a moderately soft dynamic, and crescendo-ed through to the end.

The rhythms in each bar/phrase are similar but not identical at all. The rhythm is built from standard note values (i.e. **without** triplets, double-dotted notes or syncopation, etc.). Both halves of the composition use a combination of minims, dotted crotchets and quavers (half, dotted quarter and eighth notes). The last note is held on for two bars so that the entire composition becomes eight bars in total. If I had stopped in bar 7, it would have felt a little unbalanced.

The harmonic structure of the melody is strong (see lesson 12). The chords used are (in E minor) V, I, VI, (in G major) I, V (in E minor) IV, I, II, V, I. There is a good variety, with chords I and V being used more often.

COMPOSING A MELODY FOR VOICE EXERCISES

Exercise 1

Divide each of the following texts into 8 bars. Draw bar lines between the words or syllables, in the appropriate places. Split up words of more than one syllable with a hyphen

a. Sweet, be not proud of those two eyes
    Which, star-like, sparkle in their skies.

b. Of all the birds that ever I see,
    The owl is fairest in her degree.

c. In winter, when the fields are white,
    I sing this song for your delight.

d. No stir in the air, no stir in the sea,
    The ship was as still as she could be.

Exercise 2

Write a complete melody for each of the above texts. Don't forget to include performance directions.

There is a page of blank manuscript paper at the end of this book.

COMPOSING A MELODY FOR INSTRUMENTS ANSWERS

Answers will vary. Mymusictheory.com can mark your compositions for you. Please email us at info@mymusictheory.com for more information.

Example answer for question a), written for clarinet.

Example answer for question b), written for bassoon.

Things to check for in your composition:

- Total of 8 bars. (Composition (a) should end with a bar containing the equivalent of 5 quavers (8th notes). Bar 1 is the first complete bar).
- Choice of instrument named and the m melody is within the playable range of the instrument.
- Tempo written above the stave, above the first note.
- Opening dynamic written below the stave, below the first note. Further sensitive dynamics added. Articulation added in a meaningful way.
- Final note is the tonic (G in composition (a) and D in composition (b).
- Final note is a long note (at least a crotchet (quarter note)) and falls on a strong beat.
- Rhythmic and melodic ideas from the given opening have been used to create the rest of the piece.
- A perfect cadence is implied at the end and an imperfect cadence is implied half way through.
- The rest of the harmonic foundation of the piece is satisfactory.
- There are no augmented melodic intervals.
- No two bars are identical and the rhythm/melody is not repetitious.
- The notation of the rhythm is appropriate for the time signature.

COMPOSING A MELODY FOR VOICE ANSWERS
Exercise 1

The symbol | is used to show the beginning of each bar.

a. |Sweet, be not |proud of |those two
   |eyes
   Which, |star-like, |spar-kle |in their
   |skies.

b. Of |all the |birds that |e-ver I |see,
   The |owl is |fair-est in |her de|gree.

c. In |win-ter, |when the |fields are
   |white,
   I |sing this |song for |your de-|light.

d. No |stir in the |air, no |stir in the |sea,
   The |ship was as |still as |she could
   |be.

Exercise 2

Answers will vary – an example answer is given below. MyMusictheory.com can mark your compositions for you. Please email us at info@mymusictheory.com for more information.

Things to check for in your compositions:

- The overall length is either 8 bars or 4 bars.
- The stressed syllables fall on the strongest beats of the bar.
- Words of more than one syllable are split with hyphens and set to the appropriate number of notes, and are slurred.
- The mood of the melody fits the meaning of the words.
- The composition is coherent in terms of melody and rhythm, with similarities throughout.
- The rhythm/melody is not repetitious.
- The tempo and opening dynamic are given above the first note.
- Further sensitive dynamics are given.
- The melody is harmonically coherent, with a cadence at the end.
- The melody ends on the tonic note, using a note at least the length of a crotchet (quarter note).
- The notation of the rhythm is appropriate for the time signature.
- When there is an upbeat, the final bar takes this into account.

Printed in Great Britain
by Amazon